Marks of a True Believer

Marks of a True Believer

by
John MacArthur, Jr.

WORD OF GRACE COMMUNICATIONS
P.O. Box 4000
Panorama City, CA 91412

Library of Congress Cataloging in Publication Data

MacArthur, John F.
  Marks of a true believer.

  (John MacArthur's Bible studies)
  1. Bible. N.T. Epistles of John, 1st—Criticism, interpretation, etc. 2. Identification (Religion)— Biblical teaching. I. Title. II. Series: MacArthur, John F. Bible studies.
BS2805.2.M33   1987   227'.9406   87-5603
ISBN 0-8024-5312-0

1 2 3 4 5 6 7 Printing/LC/Year 91 90 89 88 87

Printed in the United States of America

Contents

These Bible studies are taken from messages delivered by Pastor-Teacher John MacArthur, Jr., at Grace Community Church in Panorama City, California. These messages have been combined into a 6-tape album entitled *Marks of a True Believer*. You may purchase this series either in an attractive vinyl cassette album or as individual cassettes. To purchase these tapes, request the album *Marks of a True Believer*, or ask for the tapes by their individual GC numbers. Please consult the current price list; then, send your order, making your check payable to:

WORD OF GRACE COMMUNICATIONS
P.O. Box 4000
Panorama City, CA 91412

Or call the following number:
818-982-7000

1
Christians and Antichrists

Outline

Introduction
A. The Spirit of the Antichrist
B. The History of the Antichrist
   1. The Babylonian legend
   2. The Old Testament acknowledgment
     a) Isaiah 51:9
     b) Isaiah 27:1
C. The Form of the Antichrist
   1. The forerunner
   2. The final form
     a) 2 Thessalonians 2:3-4
     b) Revelation 13:1-2, 5-7
     c) Revelation 16:13
     d) Revelation 19:20
D. The Principle of the Antichrist
E. The Proliferation of Antichrists
F. The Exposure of Antichrists

Lesson
I. The Antichrists (vv. 18-19, 22-23, 26)
   A. The Introduction of the Antichrist (v. 18)
     1. The victims of false doctrine
       a) The different terms
       b) The deliberate warning
     2. The validation of Christ's presence
       a) The period
       b) The presupposition

Conclusion

Introduction

First John 2:18-27 contrasts Christians with antichrists. Verse 18 says, "Ye have heard that antichrist shall come, even now are there many antichrists, by which we know that it is the last time." That is the first time the term *antichrists* appears in the Bible. The only writer to use that word is John, and he used it only in his epistles. It appears again in verse 22: "He is antichrist, that denieth the Father and the Son." First John 4:3 says, "This is that spirit of antichrist, of which ye have heard that it should come, and even now already is it in the world." And 2 John 7 says, "This is a deceiver and an antichrist."

A. The Spirit of the Antichrist

When the Antichrist comes in the end times, he will attempt to be the Christ that men are looking for. The spirit of the Antichrist has always been in the world. It has manifested itself both in open opposition to Christ and in subtle attempts to replace Christ.

B. The History of the Antichrist

Since the Fall, mankind has sensed a power in the universe opposed to God. Apart from the Bible's revelation of Satan, men know there is good and evil in the universe.

1. The Babylonian legend

One of the earliest written records of conflict between good and evil comes from Babylonian history. The Babylonians held to a creation legend in which the god Marduk subdued an evil sea monster named Tiamat. The Babylonians believed that a final battle would occur in the end times when Tiamat would wake up and fight Marduk. That legend gives credence to the human understanding that good and evil continue to coexist and will engage in ultimate conflict. Believers know Scripture prophesies a final battle between the good and the evil.

2. The Old Testament acknowledgment

The Old Testament acknowledges the existence of such legends by its use of similar imagery.

a) Isaiah 51:9—In referring to the arm of the Lord, Isaiah said God wounded a sea monster (KJV,* "dragon"). To make his point, Isaiah borrowed from the pagan understanding that a monster represented evil in the world.

b) Isaiah 27:1—"The Lord with his hard and great and strong sword shall punish leviathan, the piercing serpent, even leviathan, that crooked serpent; and he shall slay the sea-monster that is in the sea." God will destroy evil. The concept of a serpent representing the evil came from the biblical record of Adam and Eve in the Garden, where Satan took on the form of a serpent (Gen. 3:1; cf. Rev. 12:9).

C. The Form of the Antichrist

There is an anti-God force in the world, and that force is Satan, a personal being. Often he has taken human form. There were times when Isaiah and Ezekiel were technically addressing kings but went beyond them and addressed the devil working through them. The kings were simply manifestations of the spirit of Satan.

1. The forerunner

Around 168 B.C. a man by the name of Antiochus Epiphanes came to the fore of Jewish history. Epiphanes means "the great one." He gave himself that name. The Jews called him Antiochus Epimanes, which means "the madman." Antiochus was the king of Syria. He wanted to eliminate Judaism from the earth, so he invaded Jerusalem, killed thousands of Jews, and sold others into slavery. He instituted the death penalty for anyone who circumcised a child or owned a copy of the law. He erected an altar to Zeus in the courts of the Temple. He sacrificed a pig on the altar in defiance of Jewish law. He turned the Temple chambers into brothels. All were deliberate attempts to desecrate the Temple and God. Those actions provide an appropriate picture of the coming Antichrist. Some of Daniel's proph-

*King James Version.

10

ecies of Antiochus actually refer to the future Antichrist (e.g., Dan. 11:31).

2. The final form

The anti-God force in the world has taken on many forms throughout the centuries, but there will be one great and final form.

a) 2 Thessalonians 2:3-4—"Let no man deceive you by any means; for that day [the day of the Lord] shall not come, except there come the falling away first, and that man of sin be revealed, the son of perdition, who opposeth and exalteth himself above all that is called God, or that is worshiped, so that he, as God, sitteth in the temple of God, showing himself that he is God." The day of the Lord—the time of the final judgment when Christ returns—will not occur until the Antichrist is made known. He will oppose God and exalt himself. He will sit on God's throne, passing himself off as God.

b) Revelation 13:1-2, 5-7—John, in a vision, said, "I stood upon the sand of the sea, and saw a beast rise up out of the sea, having seven heads and ten horns, and upon his horns ten crowns, and upon his heads the name of blasphemy. And the beast which I saw was like a leopard, and his feet were like the feet of a bear, and his mouth like the mouth of a lion; and the dragon [Satan] gave him his power, and his throne, and great authority. . . . There was given unto him a mouth speaking great things and blasphemies, and power was given to him to continue forty and two months [three-and-a-half years—the second half of the Tribulation]. And he opened his mouth in blasphemy against God, to blaspheme his name, and his tabernacle, and them that dwell in heaven. And it was given unto him to make war with the saints, and to overcome them; and power was given him over all kindreds, and tongues, and nations."

c) Revelation 16:13—"I saw three unclean spirits, like frogs, come out of the mouth of the dragon, and out of the mouth of the beast." Those spirits represent Satan, the Antichrist, and the false prophet.

d) Revelation 19:20—"The beast was taken, and with him the false prophet that wrought miracles before him, with which he deceived them that had received the mark of the beast, and them that worshiped his image. These both were cast alive into a lake of fire burning with brimstone." Here the beast and false prophet are cast into eternal hell. Revelation 20:10 tells us the devil will be cast in there with them.

D. The Principle of the Antichrist

The term *Antichrist* applies specifically to one man, but the term *antichrists* is broader. It basically refers to a principle of evil that is hostile and opposed to God. That principle can be incarnated in men, and such men have existed in every generation. They have either been open and blatant opponents of God and Christ, or they have made subtle attempts to replace the truth of God with their own deception.

E. The Proliferation of Antichrists

To John, *antichrists* is another word for false teachers. The Lord gave fair warning to the church about them. He said, "False Christs and false prophets shall rise, and shall show signs and wonders, to seduce, if it were possible, even the elect" (Mark 13:22). There will be a proliferation of antichrists in the last days—and that is true today. Jesus also said, "Many shall come in my name, saying, I am Christ; and shall deceive many" (Mark 13:6). Paul warned the Ephesian elders, saying, "After my departing shall grievous wolves enter in among you, not sparing the flock. Also of your own selves shall men arise, speaking perverse things" (Acts 20:29-30). There will be many deceivers, false teachers, and antichrists. Some of us aren't aware of that because our knowledge of the true Christ insulates us from them.

By the time 1 John was written, there were many antichrists: "It is the last time; and as ye have heard that antichrist shall come, even now are there many antichrists, by which we know that it is the last time" (1 John 2:18). Wherever there are Christians, there will be opposition to Christ.

F. The Exposure of Antichrists

John warned the church about antichrists. The church cannot function unless those people are exposed. A church that puts its head in the sand and doesn't deal with those who deceive and teach false doctrine will be undermined—and John knew that. So he wrote to believers in Asia, saying, "You've got to unmask the antichrists. You can't let them remain in your fellowship." Sometimes the false christ isn't in the form of a person; it's a false view of Christ.

Throughout his epistle, John gives tests for distinguishing between true and false believers. There are two basic tests: the doctrinal test and the moral test. You can identify a true Christian by his doctrine (he will confess sin and confess Christ) and by his life (he will love God and fellow believers, and he will obey the commands of God).

We see the first part of John's doctrinal test in 1 John 1:9: true believers confess their sins. The second part begins in 1 John 2:18. The primary difference between antichrists and Christians is that Christians believe in the true Christ, whereas antichrists oppose Him or substitute a false christ. The opposition is represented by the gnostic heresy that infiltrated the church in the first century. Gnostics taught that Jesus was not God in human flesh. Some thought He was only a man; others thought He was some kind of phantom. So John reaffirmed that a true Christian confesses that Jesus Christ is God in human flesh. That is his emphasis in 1 John 2:18-27. There are only two groups to consider in this passage: antichrists and Christians.

Lesson

I. THE ANTICHRISTS (vv. 18-19, 22-23, 26)

A. The Introduction of the Antichrist (v. 18)

13

"Little children, it is the last time; and as ye have heard that antichrist shall come, even now are there many antichrists, by which we know that it is the last time."

1. The victims of false doctrine

John used two different words for "little children." The Greek word he used in 1 John 2:12 and 28 is *teknia;* the one he used in verse 13 and here in verse 18 is *paidia.* What's the difference?

a) The different terms

Teknia means "offspring." It's a broad term that has nothing to do with age. However, *paidia* refers to an infant. The English word *pedagogy* comes from it, meaning "to instruct someone who is unlearned." We can conclude that John is talking to spiritual babies in verse 18.

b) The deliberate warning

John is warning spiritual babies about false teachers, because they are most susceptible to confusion. We know it is not possible for the elect to be ultimately deceived from following Christ (Matt. 24:24), but it is certainly possible for them to be confused. Why does John speak only to spiritual babies about false teachers? Because those who have matured into spiritual young men are no longer victimized by false doctrine. First John 2:14 says, "I have written unto you, young men, because ye are strong, and the word of God abideth in you." Ephesians 4:14 says the spiritually immature are "tossed to and fro, and carried about with every wind of doctrine."

2. The validation of Christ's presence

a) The period

The apostle John informs his little children that it's "the last time" (1 John 1:18). Commentators have various opinions about what that means. Some believe John was two thousand years off in his calculation. Others think he meant it was an important hour. But I believe every Christian born since then has been living in the last days. The Jews knew the Messiah would come in the last days, and they also knew there would be terrible opposition to Him. The fact that there is opposition helps to verify that Jesus is the Messiah and that it is indeed the last time.

b) The presupposition

The word *Christ* means "anointed one." It was used to translate the Hebrew word *Mashiach* (Messiah) in the Septuagint, the Greek version of the Old Testament. If there is no Christ, there can't be an antichrist. That there are antichrists in the world tells me the true Christ is here.

First John 2:18 says, "Ye have heard that antichrist shall come." Where did they hear that? Probably from their teachers, the apostles. Second Thessalonians was written long before 1 John. It is likely that John's readers had either read or heard Paul's teaching in 2 Thessalonians 2:3-12 about the coming man of sin, who would exalt himself above God, sit in the temple of God, and show himself to be God. But John adds, "Even now are there many antichrists" (1 John 2:18). Here he is referring to all deceivers and subverters of apostolic teaching. Their widespread activity is an indicator that these are the last days.

That liberal churches and cults operate without any opposition while we struggle against false teachers and deceivers is evidence to me of who is right. One of the validations of Christianity is continuing worldwide hatred of Christ and the multiplied attempts to counterfeit Him.

B. The Identification of the Antichrists (vv. 19, 22-23, 26)

John gives three characteristics of antichrists.

1. They depart from the fellowship (v. 19)

15

"They [antichrists] went out from us, but they were not of us; for if they had been of us, they would no doubt have continued with us; but they went out, that they might be made manifest that they were not all of us."

a) Their origin

Antichrists originate in the church and then depart from it. The church doesn't suffer so much from outside attacks as it does from those inside. John says antichrists left the church. Perhaps they failed to win over the leaders to their view. The churches remained unmovable because they were true to the Word. When the antichrists were unsuccessful, they bailed out. Notice John distinguishes clearly between those who left—antichrists—and those who remained—Christians.

b) Their defection

(1) Unmasking the character of the antichrists

The defection of the antichrists gives clear evidence of their true character. Their departure manifested that they were not believers. Luke 12:2 says, "There is nothing covered, that shall not be revealed; neither hidden, that shall not be known." God will unmask the deceivers.

(2) Revealing the perseverance of the saints

John said, "If they had been of us, they would . . . have continued with us" (1 John 2:19). Mark 13:20 says, "Except the Lord had shortened those days, no flesh should be saved; but for the elect's sake, whom he hath chosen, he hath shortened the days." If allowed to continue, the Tribulation could destroy even the people who are to be saved during it. So God will shorten it to make sure the elect are secured. Verse 22 says, "False Christs and false prophets shall rise, and shall show signs and wonders, to seduce, if it were possible, even the elect." There we see it isn't possible to seduce the elect. Yet Satan will continue to work through false christs to try to seduce them. God never allows anything to happen to the saints that would cause them to be lost. If someone departs the fellowship to follow false doctrine, you can be sure he was never saved. God uses his departure to manifest that fact.

Salvation is not the reward for endurance, but endurance is a mark of salvation. If the antichrists had been of us, they would have continued with us. The ultimate test of true Christianity is perseverance. True Christians remain in the fellowship.

c) Their manifestation

All will be made manifest. Some false teachers might not be manifest until the judgment, but many of them leave the fellowship, thus exposing themselves to the community of believers. People have asked me about someone they assumed to be a Christian but who has now joined a cult or become an atheist. I simply tell them to read 1 John 2:19. I'm thankful that God sent them away so that we might know the truth about them. Don't be disturbed—this knowledge isn't designed to make you doubt your security; it should give you absolute confidence because God manifests the false believers to you.

(1) Jude 19—Jude says false teachers "are they who separate themselves, sensual, having not the Spirit." If they don't have the Spirit, are they Christians? No. They separate themselves because they are false from the beginning.

(2) 1 Corinthians 11:19—Paul said, "There must be also heresies among you, that they who are approved may be made manifest among you." Heretics reveal who is true by contrast. When they depart and you stay, you can know they weren't true. You may think they were true, but that's not a judgment God wants you to make. You can't distinguish the wheat from the tares—that's why only God and His angels can separate them at the

judgment (Matt. 13:28-30). There will even be those who say, "Lord, Lord" (Matt. 7:22), but Christ will say, "I never knew you; depart from me" (v. 23). God wants the distinction clear, so He marks the phonies by their departure from the fellowship.

When you see someone who has come to church for a long time suddenly bail out in favor of some false doctrine, know that God is manifesting to us that the person was false all the time. What's even more tragic is when false believers become so comfortable in a church that eventually the true believers all leave. What remains is the typical liberal church of today—the entire fellowship is nothing but antichrists.

2. They deny the faith (vv. 22-23)

   a) The denial of the Son (v. 22a)

      "Who is a liar but he that denieth that Jesus is the Christ?"

      Anyone who denies Christ is an antichrist. All lies are alien to the truth. John has in mind the great lie—that Jesus is not the One He claimed to be. Second Thessalonians 2:11 says that during the Tribulation "God shall send . . . strong delusion, that they [unbelievers] should believe the lie." What is the lie? That Christ is not who He claimed to be. Whatever people claim to believe, if they do not believe that Jesus is God in human flesh, they are antichrists. That is John's doctrinal test—the acid test of a man's salvation.

      (1) 1 John 4:2—"By this know ye the Spirit of God: every spirit that confesseth that Jesus Christ is come in the flesh is of God; and every spirit that confesseth not that Jesus Christ is come in the flesh is not of God; and this is that spirit of antichrist . . . and even now already is it in the world." Salvation is based on one's answer to this question: Is Jesus God in human flesh?

18

(2) 2 John 7—"For many deceivers are entered into the world, who confess not that Jesus Christ cometh in the flesh." Some Gnostics said He was a phantom. The Cerinthian branch of Gnosticism said Jesus was just a man—that the Christ spirit came on Him but left. Those are the lies John was combating in his epistles. Deceivers deny the incarnation and therefore the deity of Jesus Christ. Such denial is the basis of liberalism, modernism, and the cults of today.

Certain seminaries teach that Jesus was an elevated man who had great wisdom and insight, but they deny that He is God. However, Jesus said, "Whosoever, therefore, shall confess me before men, him will I confess also before my Father, who is in heaven. But whosoever shall deny me before men, him will I also deny before my Father, who is in heaven" (Matt. 10:32-33).

b) The denial of the Father (vv. 22b-23)

"He is antichrist, that denieth the Father and the Son. Whosoever denieth the Son, the same hath not the Father; he that confesseth the Son hath the Father also."

Implicit in denying Christ is denying the Father. Some people say they believe in God in spite of not believing in Christ, but their God is not the God of the Bible because He is manifest in the Son. Anyone who denies the Son denies God. Whoever denies Christ's deity opposes the revelation that authenticates the credentials of the Messiah. To deny Jesus is to deny God. People who say they believe in God blaspheme His name by their failure to believe that Jesus Christ is God incarnate.

3. They deceive the faithful (v. 26)

"These things have I written unto you concerning them that seduce you."

Antichrists try to seduce believers. We know it's impossible for them to ultimately deceive the elect, but they try. First Timothy 4:1 says their weapons are "seducing spirits, and doctrines of demons." Satan is busy trying to seduce Christians.

The apostle John jealously guarded the welfare of Christ's sheep. He said, "I rejoiced greatly that I found of thy children walking in truth" (2 John 4). He also said, "I have no greater joy than to hear that my children walk in truth" (3 John 4). John was thrilled that the believers were secure in truth.

II. THE CHRISTIANS (vv. 20-21, 24-25, 27)

A. Their Faithfulness (vv. 20-21, 24, 27)

John presents a picture of the Christian in contrast to the antichrists. Unbelievers depart from the fellowship, deny the faith, and try to deceive the faithful. They are unsuccessful in their deception for two reasons: Christians accept the faith, and they remain faithful.

1. They accept the faith (vv. 20-21, 27)

a) The anointing of the Spirit (v. 20)

"Ye have an unction from the Holy One, and ye know all things."

(1) The words of the deceivers

Two words Gnostics commonly used to describe their religious experience were "knowledge" (Gk., *gnosis*) and "anointing" (or unction). The Gnostics would say, "We have received a special anointing of God that has given us a superior knowledge." They claimed God lifted them to a higher level of understanding.

(2) The words of the believers

John says Christians have an anointing from God Himself and that they know all things (v. 20), thus contradicting the Gnostics. It's the Christians, not the Gnostics, who have the anointing and the knowledge. The Lord has made a glorious provision for His own—He preserves them from embracing error. John had no fear that true saints would become apostate. When someone does leave the fellowship and become an apostate, it proves he never was saved. Now you might think a few of those may be Christians. But that can't be, because John says, "Ye have an [anointing] from the Holy One, and ye know all things. I have not written unto you because ye know not the truth, but because ye know it, and that no lie is of the truth" (vv. 20-21). Saints will not depart the fellowship and become apostates, because they have an anointing from the Holy One and know the truth.

(a) The role of the Spirit

The Greek word translated "unction" is *chrisma*. It is used only here and in verse 27 in the New Testament. It literally means "ointment." The anointing the believer receives is clearly the Holy Spirit. The apostle Paul said, "Now he who establisheth us with you in Christ, and hath anointed us, is God, who hath also sealed us, and given the earnest of the Spirit in our hearts" (2 Cor. 1:21-22). The believer is granted the Spirit of God as if He were an ointment, or oil, placed on him. Acts 10:38 says God anointed Jesus of Nazareth with the Holy Spirit.

(b) The role of Christ

Who is the one who anoints? According to 1 John 2:20, it's "the Holy One." That's a reference to Christ (e.g., Luke 4:34; Acts 3:14). Christ anoints the believer with the Holy Spirit. Then the Spirit gives us the knowledge of all things.

The Christian's preservative against error is the indwelling Holy Spirit. You don't need to go somewhere to pray for an anointing—you already have one. You have received the Holy Spirit, and He preserves you from error.

b) The teaching of the Spirit (vv. 21, 27)

(1) The substance of the teaching (v. 21)

"I have not written unto you because ye know not the truth, but because ye know it, and that no lie is of the truth."

How do believers come to know the truth? Christ gives the Holy Spirit to them, and He becomes their resident truth-teacher. That means knowledge of all things pertaining to spiritual truth is available to the believer through the Holy Spirit. Before Christ left the disciples He said, "The Comforter, who is the Holy Spirit, whom the Father will send in my name, he shall teach you all things, and bring all things to your remembrance" (John 14:26).

John is saying in verse 21 that the Holy Spirit teaches them that the lies of the apostates have no part with the truth. Some may fall into heresy and apostasy, and that manifests they never were saved. True believers will never fall into apostasy because the Holy Spirit is the Christian's built-in lie detector.

(2) The effect of the teaching (v. 27)

"The anointing which ye have received of him abideth in you, and ye need not that any man teach you; but as the same anointing teacheth you of all things, and is truth, and is no lie, and even as it hath taught you, ye shall abide in him."

Why does a Christian continue in Christ and not follow after false doctrine? Because of the teaching ministry of the Holy Spirit. God has so en-

22

dowed the Christian with discernment that he ultimately will not be deceived by lies. He may become confused at times, but he will always abide in Christ. He won't decide in favor of false doctrine because he can't. Verse 27 speaks of "the anointing which ye have received of him." That statement is in the past tense—you received the Spirit when you were saved, and he continues to abide in you (Rom. 8:9). The Spirit never leaves a Christian; true Christians never depart from the faith. If they ever did, the Holy Spirit would have failed in His ministry of teaching the truth.

Do We Need Human Teachers?

What did John mean when he said, "Ye need not that any man teach you"? Obviously it doesn't mean we shouldn't have a human teacher. The Lord has given teachers to the church. First Corinthians 12:28 refers to those who have the gift of teaching. John is not saying we don't need human teachers; he is saying we don't need human *teaching*. We are not to be dependent on human wisdom but on God's Word, whether it's taught by spirit-filled human teachers or the Spirit Himself as He works on our hearts. The thing we don't need is human teachers teaching human philosophy. We need Spirit-filled teachers.

Antichrists will deny the faith and try to deceive the faithful. But the true Christian has the anointing of the Holy Spirit to preserve him from error. He will never defect. He may get tossed around a little, but he will never leave, because Christians accept the faith through the Holy Spirit.

2. They remain faithful (v. 24)

"Let that, therefore, abide in you which ye have heard from the beginning. If that which ye have heard from the beginning shall remain in you, ye also shall continue in the Son, and in the Father."

a) The effort

You need to consciously hold to the truth—to contend for the faith (Jude 3)—and the Holy Spirit will make sure that you do. It is your responsibility to contend for the faith with all your being, and it is the Spirit's responsibility to keep holding onto you. I wouldn't need to preach a sermon or write a book if all you had to do was let the Holy Spirit keep you from error. We must be involved. That dichotomy occurs in every aspect of the Christian life.

The three English words *abide, remain,* and *continue* are all translated from the same Greek word *menō,* which refers to continued dwelling. John is saying that if you continue in what you have heard, then what you have heard will continue in you. Our part is to continue abiding in God's Word; the Spirit's part is to keep us.

b) The exhortations

True Christians hold to the faith and tenaciously defend the truth.

(1) 1 Corinthians 15:1-2—"Moreover, brethren, I declare unto you the gospel which I preached unto you, which also ye have received, and in which ye stand; by which also ye are saved, if ye keep in memory what I preached unto you."

(2) John 8:31—Jesus said, "If ye continue in my word, then are ye my disciples indeed."

(3) Colossians 1:22-23—Paul said Christ will "present you holy and unblamable and unreprovable in his sight, if ye continue in the faith grounded and settled, and be not moved away from the hope of the gospel, which ye have heard, and which was preached to every creature that is under heaven."

(4) 2 Timothy 3:14—"Continue thou in the things which thou hast learned."

The Word of God is clear: the Christian life is not automatic. It is true that the Holy Spirit secures us and guarantees us against defection. But at the same time the Bible instructs us to fight for the faith and continue in the Word. The contrast is simple: true Christians hold to the faith; antichrists deny it.

B. Their Future (v. 25)

"This is the promise that he hath promised us, even eternal life."

That is the future of Christians. What is the end of antichrists? Read 2 Peter 2.

Conclusion

Christians have two safeguards against heresy: the Holy Spirit and God's Word. The Holy Spirit is doing His part. Your part is to be obedient to Scripture. In some cases true believers drift away from the fellowship for a little while, but they are drawn back. There may even be some believers who drift away and die before they come back. God may have had to discipline them—He alone knows whether they're genuine or not. But the majority who depart from the fellowship were never believers to begin with. What about you? Are you a phony who will depart some day? Or are you a genuine Christian who has been secured by the Spirit and is continuing in the faith?

Focusing on the Facts

1. What will the Antichrist try to do during the end times (see p. 9)?
2. Who is behind the anti-God force in the world (see p. 10)?
3. Who was Antiochus Epiphanes? Who does he picture (see p. 10)?
4. Explain the difference between the terms *Antichrist* and *antichrists* (see p. 12).
5. Describe the warning Christ gave the church about antichrists (see p. 12).

6. What will happen to a church that doesn't deal with false teachers (see p. 13)?
7. What are John's two tests for distinguishing between true and false believers? What will those tests manifest (see p. 13)?
8. Explain the difference between the two Greek words John uses for children (see p. 14).
9. Who needs to be warned about false teaching (see p. 14)?
10. What period does "the last time" refer to (1 John 2:18; see pp. 14-15)?
11. What does the name *Christ* mean (see p. 15)?
12. How can we know Christ is real by what is happening in the world today (see p. 15)?
13. What three characteristics identify antichrists (1 John 2:19, 22-23, 26; see pp. 15-19)?
14. What is the origin of antichrists (see p. 16)?
15. What is the ultimate test of true Christianity? Why (see p. 17)?
16. What do people manifest about themselves when they leave the fellowship of the church to follow false doctrine (see pp. 17-18)?
17. What is the great lie (see p. 18)?
18. What is implied in the denial of Christ as God (1 John 2:22b-23; see p. 19)?
19. Why are antichrists unable to deceive believers (see p. 20)?
20. What two words did the heretics of John's day use to describe their religious experience? How did John use those words to denounce them (1 John 2:20; see p. 20)?
21. What is the anointing that the believer receives? Who does the anointing (see p. 21)?
22. In what sense can the Holy Spirit be considered the believer's built-in lie detector (see p. 22)?
23. Why do Christians need human teachers (see p. 23)?
24. What responsibility does the Holy Spirit have regarding the Christian's faith? What is the believer's responsibility (see p. 24)?

Pondering the Principles

1. In his first epistle the apostle John gives tests that distinguish the true from the false. There are basically two tests: doctrinal and moral. The doctrinal test tells us that a true Christian will confess sin and confess Christ as Lord. The moral test tells us that a true Christian will love God and his fellow believers, and

he will obey the commands of God. To understand how John used those tests in the first part of his epistle, read 1 John 1:1–2:17. Record every verse that refers to one of the two tests. Next to each verse indicate which test is discussed and which specific aspect of the test is covered.

2. In 1 John 2:12-14 John shows us there are three levels of growth in the Christian life: children, young men, and fathers. What are the distinguishing characteristics between the three? At which level would you place yourself? If you consider yourself to be a spiritual child, what are you doing to further your knowledge of the truth? If you are not daily spending time in reading and studying God's Word, you won't ever reach the level of a young man. For those of you who consider yourselves to be young men or fathers, what are you doing to help the spiritually immature to grow into a greater knowledge of the truth? Seek out those who need your help, and make a commitment to pour your life into them.

3. According to 1 John 2:20, 27, the Holy Spirit teaches us the truth, which in turn helps us to identify error. In what ways has the Holy Spirit taught you the difference between truth and error? Be specific. Thank God for His provision of the Holy Spirit's teaching ministry in you. Ask Him to continue to guide you into the truth.

4. Although you have supernatural help in your resistance to false doctrine, you also are responsible to consciously fight for the truth (Jude 3). In what ways have you been contending for the faith? In what areas have you been depending on the Holy Spirit only? Take a closer look at those areas. What are some things you can do to be better equipped to resist false doctrine? (For example, if you don't know much about what certain cults teach, read some books about them.) Remember, the Holy Spirit will ultimately keep you from error, but you need to make the commitment to be ready to defend the faith.

2
The Purifying Hope

Outline

Introduction
A. The Characteristics of Hope
B. The Compulsion of Hope

Lesson
I. Hope Is Guaranteed by Abiding (2:28)
   A. The Recipients of the Command (v. 28*a*)
   B. The Reality of Confidence (v. 28*b*)
      1. The appearance of Christ
      2. The assurance of Christians
         a) A confident boldness
         b) An unashamed blamelessness
            (1) The shame of the world
               (*a*) Revelation 6:15-17
               (*b*) Daniel 12:2
               (*c*) Mark 8:38
            (2) The holiness of the saints
               (*a*) Ephesians 5:25-27
               (*b*) Colossians 1:22
               (*c*) 1 Thessalonians 3:13
               (*d*) 1 Thessalonians 5:23
II. Hope Is Realized in Righteousness (2:29)
   A. Unmasking the Phonies
   B. Understanding Righteousness
      1. 1 Peter 1:14-16
      2. 2 Corinthians 13:5

III. Hope Is Established by Love (3:1)
   A. The Manner of God's Love
      1. Identified
      2. Illustrated
         a) Matthew 8:24-27
         b) 2 Peter 3:10-11
   B. The Orientation of God's Love
      1. Human love
      2. God's love
   C. The Result of God's Love
   D. The Hatred of God's Love
IV. Hope Is Fulfilled in Christlikeness (3:2)
   A. Being Like Children (v. 2*a*)
   B. Being Like Christ (v. 2*b*)
      1. Romans 8:29
      2. Revelation 22:4
      3. Philippians 3:20-21
V. Hope Is Characterized by Purity (3:3)

Introduction

A. The Characteristics of Hope

The Bible talks a great deal about hope.

1. Hope is in God

Our hope is to be in God and in God alone. Psalm 43:5 says, "Why art thou cast down, O my soul? And why art thou disquieted within me? Hope in God; for I shall yet praise him, who is the health of my countenance, and my God." God is our only refuge, resource, and hope. Psalm 78:7 says, "That they might set their hope in God, and not forget the works of God." We can trust God for the future because of what He has done in the past and present.

2. Hope is a gift from God

Second Thessalonians 2:16 says, "Our Lord Jesus Christ himself, and God, even our Father . . . hath loved us, and hath given us everlasting consolation and good hope through grace." God grants men hope, confidence, assurance, and security in the future if they will accept them as a gift.

3. Hope comes from Scripture

When you understand and believe the Word of God, you will have hope. Romans 15:4 says, "Whatever things were written in earlier times [the Old Testament] were written for our learning, that we, through patience and comfort of the scriptures, might have hope." If you don't believe the Bible, you will lack hope and confidence in the future.

4. Hope is secured by Christ's resurrection

We can believe God when He tells us that we can trust in Him to have victory over death. But Christ's death and resurrection assure us all the more. We know by example that it is possible to conquer death. First Peter 1:3 says, "Blessed be the God and Father of our Lord Jesus Christ, who, according to His abundant mercy, hath begotten us again unto a living hope by the resurrection of Jesus Christ from the dead."

5. Hope is confirmed by the Holy Spirit

Romans 15:13 says, "The God of hope fill you with all joy and peace in believing, that ye may abound in hope, through the power of the Holy Spirit." One of the ministries of the Holy Spirit is to convince the believer that he has hope for the future.

6. Hope is a defense against Satan

When the Holy Spirit confirms hope in the believer, it acts as a defense against Satan. The devil is always trying to make us doubt and worry about the future. He'll say, "How do you know you're really saved?" But when the Holy Spirit confirms our hope, we won't fall prey to Satan's attacks. First Thessalonians 5:8 says, "Let us, who are of the day, be sober, putting on the breastplate of faith and love, and, for an helmet, the hope of salvation." Satan wants to split you wide open with his great broadsword of doubt, but you have the helmet of the hope of salvation to protect you against his blows.

7. Hope is to be continual

The believer should never lose hope. Psalm 71:14 says, "I will hope continually, and will yet praise thee more and more." The psalmist wrote this in his old age. He is an example to us because he did not lose hope through the years.

8. Hope produces joy

Psalm 146:5 says, "Happy is he that hath the God of Jacob for his help, whose hope is in the Lord, his God."

9. Hope removes the fear of death

When we truly hope in God and Christ, there is nothing to fear. Colossians 1:5 says the believer's hope is laid up in heaven. There is coming a day when we will meet the Lord and receive this promise: "You . . . hath he reconciled . . . to present you holy and unblamable and unreprovable in his sight, if ye continue in the faith grounded and settled, and be not moved away from the hope of the gospel, which ye have heard, and which was preached to every creature that is under heaven, of which I, Paul, am made a minister" (Col. 1:21-23). Verse 27 says, "To whom God would make known what is the riches of the glory of the mystery among the Gentiles, which is Christ in you, the hope of glory." We have hope for the future because Christ resides in us now. In 1 Corinthians 15:20 Paul indicates we have hope because of Christ's resurrection. Christ is our hope, and the fear of death has been removed.

10. Hope is secure

Nothing can take away the believer's hope. Hebrews 6:18 says, "By two immutable things [two things that can't change—God made a promise and He swore by it], in which it was impossible for God to lie, we might have a strong consolation, who have fled for refuge to lay hold upon the hope set before us." Our hope is secure because God established the oath. And because of who He is, we know He will never break it. He can't lie. Verse 19 says our hope is "an anchor of the soul, both sure and steadfast, and which entereth into that within the veil." Christ attached the anchor of hope directly to the throne of God. That's how secure our hope is.

11. Hope is fulfilled in Christ's return

Titus 2:13 says, "Looking for that blessed hope, and the glorious appearing of the great God and our Savior, Jesus Christ." Jesus is coming; therein lies the fulfillment of our hope.

12. Hope is purifying

Hope for the future has a tremendous effect on the present. First John 3:3 says, "Every man that hath this hope in him [Christ] purifieth himself even as he [Christ] is pure." John is saying hope in Christ has a purifying effect. Our hope isn't just theological; it's ethical—it has behavioral consequences. If I believe Christ is coming again and that I will be brought before His judgment seat, that will make a difference in the way I behave. Paul said there's a crown of righteousness laid up in heaven for all who "love his appearing" (2 Tim. 4:8). That means you love the second coming enough to do something about it.

B. The Compulsion of Hope

John uses the concept of purifying hope to reiterate and elaborate on his moral test for determining a true Christian. If a person is a Christian, he will have hope in the return of Christ, and that hope will affect his behavior. He will live a pure life. There were people in the church who said they believed in Christ, but there was no purity in their lives. John identified them as phonies. The proof of being a Christian is not just having a hope but in having a hope that makes a difference in your life.

There are five features of the believer's hope in 1 John 2:28–3:3.

I. HOPE IS GUARANTEED BY ABIDING (2:28)

Abiding refers to a permanent relationship with Christ, which is the measure of a true believer. John 8:31 says, "If ye continue in my word, then are ye my disciples indeed." (See pp. 22-24 for the discussion of abiding.)

A. The Recipients of the Command (v. 28a)

"And now, little children, abide in him."

In verse 27 John says, "Ye shall abide in him," which is a present-indicative statement: you are abiding. But in verse 28 he commands the believers to abide in Him. If they already are abiding, why do they need to be commanded to do so? John begins by addressing his readers as "little children" (Gk., *teknion*, a reference to children in general). John is not referring to spiritual babies anymore; he is talking to all the children of God. He has finished his instruction for the babes, the young men, and the fathers (1 John 2:13-27). So John is telling all believers to abide in Christ. Abiding guarantees hope. To continue in the faith is the work of the Spirit, but it's the believer's responsibility to hold to the truth.

B. The Reality of Confidence (v. 28b)

"When he shall appear, we may have confidence and not be ashamed before him at his coming."

1. The appearance of Christ

The Greek word translated "appear" is *phaneroō*, which means "to be made manifest" or "to be made visible." It's used many places in reference to Christ—to His incarnation (1 Tim. 3:16), His resurrection (John 21:1, 14), and His return (Col. 3:4). But 1 John 2:28 refers to the rapture. Jesus is coming for His church. When He does, He will be made visible. Right now He is invisible. Peter

34

said, "Whom, having not seen, ye love" (1 Pet. 1:8). We haven't seen Him, but we love Him, and we look forward to the day when we will see Him.

2. The assurance of Christians

When that day comes, John says true Christians will "have confidence and not be ashamed before him at his coming [Gk., *parousia*, "to be beside"]." Those who abide in Christ won't be ashamed when He comes. All the mistakes believers have made are taken care of in the blood of Christ. As a result, we will have boldness. The Greek word translated "confidence" (*parrhēsia*) literally means "boldness."

The Rewards for the Church

What will happen when Jesus comes? Revelation 22:12 says, "Behold, I come quickly, and my reward is with me, to give every man according as his work shall be." The first thing Jesus will do when He comes for His church is to reward His people for their service. We will be able to go before the judgment seat of Christ with absolute confidence. How can we have that confidence? Because we are saved.

1. 2 Timothy 4:6-8—Paul said, "I am now ready to be offered, and the time of my departure is at hand. I have fought a good fight, I have finished my course, I have kept the faith; henceforth there is laid up for me a crown of righteousness, which the Lord, the righteous judge, shall give me at that day [the day Jesus is manifest to His church]; and not to me only, but unto all them also that love his appearing." Christians have something special to look forward to because of their service to Christ.

2. 2 Corinthians 5:10—"We must all appear before the judgment seat of Christ." The *bēma* (judgment seat) has nothing to do with condemnation; it serves only for giving out rewards. There's no condemnation to those who are in Christ (Rom. 8:1). Verse 10 adds that everyone will receive a reward—no one will be ashamed.

3. 1 Corinthians 3:12-15—You can spend your life piling up wood, hay, and stubble—the kinds of things that don't accomplish

35

anything. Build up gold, silver, and precious stones on the foundation of your Christian life. Those things stand the test of fire and will result in rewards.

4. 1 Corinthians 4:5—Paul said we're to "judge nothing before the time, until the Lord come, who both will bring to light the hidden things of darkness, and will make manifest the counsels of the hearts; and then shall every man have praise of God." Every individual at the judgment seat of Christ will have praise from God. There is no shame for anyone. It is true that someone may have less than someone else, but that won't be any cause for shame.

In 2 John 8 the apostle John warns believers about rewards: "Look to yourselves, that we lose not those things which we have wrought, but that we receive a full reward." You can lose a reward by not being faithful to obey God's Word. Those who abide in Christ will have confidence when they see Him. I can approach the judgment seat of Christ with boldness because He has taken care of my sin. I'm not out to rack up rewards, but I do want to show Christ that I'm faithful.

a) A confident boldness

As we've noted before, the Greek word translated "confidence" in 1 John 2:28 refers to outspokenness or freedom of speech. The same word is used in Hebrews 4:16: "Let us, therefore, come boldly unto the throne of grace." You can approach God boldly because you are without blemish and spot on account of the blood of Christ.

The same boldness is available to us in prayer. First John 3:21-22 says, "If our heart condemn us not, then have we confidence toward God. And whatever we ask, we receive of him." And 1 John 5:14 says, "This is the confidence that we have in him, that, if we ask any thing according to his will, he heareth us; and if we know that he hear us, whatever we ask, we know that we have the petitions that we desired of him." The same confidence I have to enter the holy of holies by the blood of Christ allows me to approach the judgment seat of Christ without shame.

b) An unashamed blamelessness

(1) The shame of the world

First John 2:28 indicates that some people will be ashamed when Christ returns: "We may have confidence and not be ashamed." The people who choose not to follow Christ will be ashamed when He comes.

(*a*) Revelation 6:15-17—"The kings of the earth, and the great men, and the rich men, and the chief captains, and the mighty men, and every slave, and every free man, hid themselves in the dens and in the rocks of the mountains, and said to the mountains and rocks, Fall on us, and hide us from the face of him that sitteth on the throne, and from the wrath of the Lamb; for the great day of his wrath is come, and who shall be able to stand?" They were ashamed. On that great day in the future, the searchlight of divine holiness will be pointed at two radically different classes of people.

(*b*) Daniel 12:2—"Many of those who sleep in the dust of the earth shall awake, some to everlasting life, and some to shame and everlasting contempt."

(*c*) Mark 8:38—"Whosoever, therefore, shall be ashamed of me and of my words in this adulterous and sinful generation, of him also shall the Son of man be ashamed, when he cometh in the glory of his Father, with the holy angels." The ones who will be ashamed when Jesus comes are those who were ashamed of Him and His Word in this age.

(2) The holiness of the saints

The true Christian is not ashamed of Jesus Christ and His Word. If you abide in Him, you won't be ashamed when He comes. My hope is guaranteed because I hold to Christ, so I know I will stand before Him with boldness.

(a) Ephesians 5:25-27—"Christ also loved the church, and gave himself for it, that he might sanctify and cleanse it with the washing of water by the word; that he might present it to himself a glorious church, not having spot, or wrinkle, or any such thing; but that it should be holy and without blemish."

(b) Colossians 1:22—"In the body of his flesh through death, [He died] to present you holy and unblamable and unreprovable in his sight."

(c) 1 Thessalonians 3:13—"To the end he may establish your hearts unblamable in holiness before God."

(d) 1 Thessalonians 5:23—"The very God of peace sanctify you wholly; and I pray God your whole spirit and soul and body be preserved blameless unto the coming of our Lord Jesus Christ. Faithful is he that calleth you, who also will do it."

We have a great hope, and that hope is guaranteed as we abide in Christ.

II. HOPE IS REALIZED IN RIGHTEOUSNESS (2:29)

"If ye know that he is righteous, ye know that everyone that doeth righteousness is born of him."

Our hope is made visible by our pattern of life. People who have hope live righteously because right theology produces right behavior.

A. Unmasking the Phonies

John unmasks the Gnostics in verse 29. They claimed to be born of God, but if that were true, they would be righteous like God because children tend to be like their parents.

People born of God have a righteous life-style. They have an incorruptible seed within them that must produce a righteous life (1 Pet. 1:23). The phonies proved they didn't have that seed by their unrighteous living.

B. Understanding Righteousness

In verse 29 John says, "If ye know [Gk., *oida*, "to know absolutely"] that He is righteous, ye know [Gk., *ginosko*, "to know by experience"] that everyone that doeth righteousness is born of him." That verse is a spiritual axiom. Psalm 11:7 says, "The righteous Lord loveth righteousness." God is righteous: He is innocent of any evil, and He always does right and makes right judgments. If that is characteristic of Him, you would expect His children to behave in the same manner.

1. 1 Peter 1:14-16—Peter tells believers they shouldn't act as they did before they were Christians: "As obedient children, not fashioning yourselves according to the former lusts in your ignorance but, as he who hath called you is holy, so be ye holy in all manner of life, because it is written, Be ye holy; for I am holy." If He who begot us is holy, then we who are begotten of Him will manifest that same righteousness.

2. 2 Corinthians 13:5—Paul said this to the Corinthians: "Examine yourselves, whether you are in the faith." How would you examine yourself? Look at your works —your fruit.

Our hope is realized by a righteous life. Those who claim to know God but don't live righteously discredit their claim by their life-style. True hope will result in a righteous life.

III. HOPE IS ESTABLISHED BY LOVE (3:1)

"Behold, what manner of love the Father hath bestowed upon us, that we should be called the children of God; therefore, the world knoweth us not, because it knew him not."

A. The Manner of God's Love

1. Identified

Why does John describe God's love as "what manner of love"? Perhaps he tried to call it super, colossal, stupendous, magnanimous, or unbelievable but eventually gave up. Just the concept of God's love overwhelmed John. He might have understood it better had God called believers slaves, neighbors, or friends. But to be called God's actual children was more wonderful than John could imagine. Hebrews 2:11 says Jesus is not ashamed to call us His brothers. We cry to God, "Abba, Father" (Rom. 8:15). Our hope is predicated and built on His love.

The phrase translated "what manner" (*potapēn*) in classical Greek referred to a country, race, or tribe. It referred to something foreign. So John is saying, "What kind of foreign love did God bestow on us to make us His sons?" The love of God is foreign to the human race. It is otherworldly. It belongs in a different dimension.

2. Illustrated

a) Matthew 8:24-27—The disciples had a problem—a storm on the sea: "There arose a great tempest in the sea, insomuch that the boat was covered with the waves; but he [Jesus] was asleep. And his disciples came to him, and awoke him, saying, Lord, save us; we perish. And He saith unto them, Why are ye fearful, O ye of little faith? Then he arose, and rebuked the winds and the sea; and there was a great calm. But the men marveled, saying, What manner (Gk., *potapēn*) of man is this, that even the winds and the sea obey him?" The same word used in 1 John 3:1 to describe God's love is used here to describe Jesus.

b) 2 Peter 3:10-11—"The day of the Lord will come as a thief in the night, in which the heavens shall pass away with a great noise, and the elements shall melt with fervent heat; the earth also, and the works that are in it, shall be burned up. Seeing, then, that all these things shall be dissolved, what manner of persons ought you to be in all holy living and godliness?" Since we're God's children, and we know how the world is going to end, we ought to be otherworldly people. Why would you want to attach yourself to something that is going to burn up?

God loved us with an unearthly love—a love the world can't relate to. Jesus was an unearthly person, and we are to be unearthly people.

B. The Orientation of God's Love

1. Human love

God's love for us is not object-oriented, but human love often is. Human love discriminates on the basis of the object's attraction.

2. God's love

God's love has nothing to do with the object. The Bible says that God Himself is love (1 John 4:8). His love is indiscriminate—it is based on His nature. God loved the apostle John not because John was a great person, but because it was His nature to love. His love provided the gift of salvation (John 3:16). It's not object oriented; it's free (Rom. 6:23).

C. The Result of God's Love

God's love resulted in our being called the children of God. It's exciting to realize that God is my Father. I can go to Him as I can to my human father. If I ask Him for bread, He won't give me a stone, because He loves me (Matt. 7:9). Romans 8:17 says we are joint heirs with Christ. God is going to allow us to share in everything He has prepared for Christ.

The story of the prodigal son is a sad story with a happy ending. According to Luke 15:11-13, a young man told his father he was leaving home. He took his inheritance and wasted it. Eventually, He found himself slopping hogs so that he could eat. He realized that what his father's servants had was better than what he was enduring. So he returned home. When his father saw him returning, he ran out and hugged and kissed him. The son said, "Father, I have sinned against heaven, and before thee, and am no more worthy to be called thy son; make me as one of thy hired servants" (vv. 18-19). But his father took him back as his son, put a ring on his hand, gave him the best robe, killed a fattened calf, and said his son had returned (vv. 22-24). God has made you a son, not a slave.

D. The Hatred of God's Love

John adds in 1 John 3:1: "The world knoweth us not, because it knew him not." Jesus was otherworldly, and so are we. No wonder the world doesn't know us. In John 15:18 Jesus says, "If the world hate you, ye know that it hated me before it hated you."

IV. HOPE IS FULFILLED IN CHRISTLIKENESS (3:2)

A. Being Like Children (v. 2a)

"Beloved, now are we the children of God."

When did you become a child of God? The minute you believed. If you are a believer, you are a child of God now, although you may be somewhat disappointed in what God has produced so far. That reminds me of a story about a little boy in a junior Sunday school class who poked and hit other kids. The teacher was talking about God as Creator when he asked this boy, "Who made you?" The little boy said, "God did." The teacher said, "Well, He didn't do a very good job." The little boy said, "That's because He ain't finished yet." How true! God isn't finished with us yet. What is now a process will become an instantaneous accomplishment when Jesus comes again.

However, I'm still God's child right now. The biggest change has already happened in my life. Death won't change me much; it is simply my transference into His heavenly presence. We aren't wearing our white robes or our crowns yet; we're still struggling against the flesh and the devil. We live in a sinful world, and we struggle with mortal weakness, but we're no less the sons of God.

We are like a sculpture that God continues to chisel as more and more of our form emerges. Michelangelo said that in every block of stone he saw an angel waiting to be liberated. God looks at us and says, "There's something in there, and I'm going to get it out!"

B. Being Like Christ (v. 2b)

"It doth not yet appear what we shall be, but we know that, when he shall appear, we shall be like him; for we shall see him as he is."

God's plan is to make every Christian like Christ.

1. Romans 8:29—"Whom he did foreknow, he also did predestinate to be conformed to the image of his Son." Every Christian is going to be like Christ. John 17:24 and 1 Corinthians 13:12 promise that we will see His glory.

2. Revelation 22:4—"They shall see his face; and his name shall be in their foreheads." We will see Jesus face-to-face for all eternity. When we see Him, we'll become like Him.

3. Philippians 3:20-21—"We look for the Savior, the Lord Jesus Christ, who shall change our lowly body, that it may be fashioned like his glorious body."

A Glorious Body Like Christ's

What is Christ's glorious body like? After the resurrection, Jesus was able to walk through walls. He also was able to eat (Luke 24:36-43). We will do what He could do. Jesus gave us an illustration of what a glorified body is like.

1. An incorruptible body

First Corinthians 15:42 says about our resurrection bodies: "It is sown in corruption; it is raised in incorruption." An incorruptible body has no decay—it never grows old. Our present bodies are corruptible but one day will become incorruptible.

2. A glorified body

Verse 43 says, "It is sown in dishonor; it is raised in glory." Our bodies will be glorified. There's nothing honorable about a body decaying in the grave. But our bodies will transcend anything we can dream of.

3. A powerful body

Verse 43 also says, "It is sown in weakness; it is raised in power." Our bodies will be so powerful that we will descend out of heaven with Christ when He returns to the earth (Rev. 19:14).

4. A spiritual body

Verse 44 says, "It is sown a natural body; it is raised a spiritual body." Our bodies will be governed by the Spirit, not the flesh.

Our resurrection bodies will be just like the Lord's. His resurrection body was spiritual—it was not confined to the natural world. His body was powerful; He ascended into heaven. He was glorified. And His body was incorruptible. Since all those things were true of Him, they'll be true of you.

V. HOPE IS CHARACTERIZED BY PURITY (3:3)

"Every man that hath this hope in him purifieth himself even as he is pure."

If you know that someday you'll be like Christ, that builds within you a desire to become like Him now. We all operate on the basis of motive, and knowing that Jesus is coming ought to motivate you. Just before Jesus ascended into heaven He told the disciples that they would be His witnesses (Acts 1:8). As the disciples watched Him ascend, two angels appeared and said, "Ye men of Galilee, why stand ye gazing up into heaven? This same Jesus, who is taken up from you into heaven, shall so come in like manner" (Acts 1:11). Why did the angels say that? To motivate the disciples to serve Him because He is coming back. Our lives ought to be purified by the knowledge of His return. When Jesus comes back, what would you like Him to find you doing? Serving and loving Him? If you believe

He is coming to give you rewards and make you like Himself, that is motive enough to make you purify your life.

Motive is a strong influence in our lives. We're motivated all the time. People on television motivate us. We're motivated by the presence of authority figures. When we drive we watch for police cars. Children are motivated by the teacher in the classroom or the arrival of their parents on the scene of some forbidden activity. I remember the days when I played football and at the end of practice we were required to do push-ups. Whenever the coach's back was turned no one did any, but as soon as he looked, we were all huffing and puffing. The presence of an authority figure changes the way we behave. But Jesus isn't just an authority figure to us; He's our loving Savior who is coming to reward us and to make us like Himself. That should produce in us the kind of love and gratitude that causes us to respond in obedience and conformity to His pure standard.

Focusing on the Facts

1. What does the Bible teach about hope (see pp. 30-33)?
2. Explain how hope in the future has an effect on the present (1 John 3:3; see p. 33).
3. Why did the apostle John command believers to abide when he previously told them they were already abiding (1 John 2:27-28; see p. 34)?
4. What will Christ do for believers when He comes (see p. 35)?
5. Why can believers approach God boldly (see p. 36)?
6. Who will be ashamed when Christ returns (see p. 37)?
7. What manifests the hope of the believer (1 John 2:29; see p. 38)?
8. Since God is righteous, what should be expected of His children (see pp. 38-39)?
9. Explain the meaning of the phrase "what manner" in 1 John 3:1 (see p. 40).
10. Explain the difference between God's love and human love (see p. 41).
11. According to Romans 8:29, what is God's plan for every Christian (see p. 43)?
12. Describe a resurrected body (see pp. 43-44).

13. What should motivate Christians to be like Christ in their daily lives (1 John 3:3; see p. 44)?

Pondering the Principles

1. Review the section on what the Bible says about hope (see pp. 30-33). How does each of those truths increase your hope? Be specific.

2. The believer's hope is guaranteed by abiding, realized in righteousness, established by love, fulfilled in Christlikeness, and characterized by purity. On a scale of 1-10, rate the effectiveness of your life-style in each of those areas. Which one are you the weakest in? Commit yourself this week to strengthen that area of your life. Be obedient, and see if your trust in God improves.

3
Why Christians and Sin Are Incompatible

Outline

Introduction
A. The Key Verse
    1. The parts of the moral test
    2. The violation of the moral test
        a) The argument of the Gnostics
        b) The argument of John
B. The Critical Statements
    1. Apparent contradictions
    2. Alternative explanations

Lesson
I. Sin Is Incompatible with the Law of God (v. 4)
    A. The Definitions of Sin
    B. The Delight of God's Law
        1. Scrutinized
            a) Psalm 119
            b) Romans 6:16-18
            c) Hebrews 8:10
            d) Romans 7:15-16, 22-24
        2. Simplified
            a) Romans 13:8
            b) Galatians 5:14
            c) Galatians 6:2
II. Sin Is Incompatible with the Work of Christ (vv. 5-8)
    A. Christ's Removal of Sin (v. 5)
        1. His success
            a) Ephesians 5:25-27
            b) Titus 2:14
        2. His sinlessness

B. Christ's Union with Believers (vv. 6-7)
  1. The righteousness of believers
    a) Illustrated
      (1) The resurrection to new life
      (2) The result of new life
    b) Illuminated
  2. A reminder of the deception
C. Christ's Destruction of Satan (v. 8)
  1. The source of sin
  2. The scope of destruction
    a) Satan's works
    b) Satan's life
III. Sin Is Incompatible with the Ministry of the Spirit (v. 9)
  A. The Acquisition of the Seed
  B. The Work of the Spirit
    1. 1 Peter 1:22-23
    2. 2 Peter 1:3-4

Conclusion

Introduction

The primary purpose of 1 John is to expose Gnostic false teachers existing among the believers in the church. They were confusing them with their claims to be true Christians and true teachers, which they were not. John was concerned that Christians know how to determine the true from the false before they became victimized by their false doctrine. He presents two tests believers can use to determine the validity of anyone's claim to be a Christian: the doctrinal test and the moral test. Those tests are the dominant theme of all five chapters of 1 John.

A. The Key Verse

First John 3:10 is the key to verses 4-10: "In this the children of God are manifest, and the children of the devil: whosoever doeth not righteousness is not of God, neither he that loveth not his brother."

1. The parts of the moral test

   Verse 10 contains the two parts of the moral test: a true Christian does righteous deeds and loves his brothers. The children of the devil don't do either one. Verses 4-10 talk about righteousness, and verses 11-24 talk about loving the brothers. Practicing righteousness and loving the brothers are not new themes to John—he dealt with both in 1 John 1-2. But beginning with chapter 3 and extending to the end of the epistle, John places greater importance on them. His thesis is this: a believer, a true child of God, will manifest proper doctrine and proper behavior.

2. The violation of the moral test

   A group called the Gnostics claimed to have a supernatural knowledge that belonged only to them, but they were heretics. As many others, they claimed to be Christians, yet habitually practiced sin. In addition, they lorded their superior knowledge over everyone else, proving they had no love for others. They violated both parts of the moral test.

   a) The argument of the Gnostics

      John addresses the Gnostic error regarding sin in verses 4-10. The Gnostics claimed that man is divided into a philosophical dualism: the flesh and the spirit. They said that the body is evil and that there's nothing anyone can do to change it, so we might as well let it fulfill its lusts. But they said the soul is different—that it is totally detached from the body—so it suffers none of the consequences of sin. They believed a person could sin all he wanted to without its ever affecting him.

   b) The argument of John

      However, John said true Christianity and sin are incompatible. A person cannot claim to be a Christian and go on sinning. A person who is in fellowship with God, who is saved, who is born into God's family, has the desire to avoid sin and has a new nature with the ability to avoid it. The Christian's identity as a son of God means there will be a behavioral manifestation of his sonship.

B. The Critical Statements

There are two critical statements in 1 John 3:4-10. The first is in verse 6 and the second in verse 9. Verse 6 says, "Whosoever abideth in him sinneth not." Verse 9 says, "Whosoever is born of God doth not commit sin." Verse 6 says sin is inappropriate for a Christian; verse 9 says it is impossible for a Christian.

1. Apparent contradictions

Verse 9 has startled many people. How can John possibly say a Christian doesn't sin? I know a lot of them, and they sin; I'm a Christian, and I sin. Verse 9 apparently contradicts 1 John 1:8-10: "If we say that we have no sin, we deceive ourselves, and the truth is not in us. If we confess our sins, he is faithful and just to forgive us our sins, and to cleanse us from all unrighteousness. If we say that we have not sinned, we make him a liar, and his word is not in us."

What is the answer to this dilemma? Can a Christian sin? How much can a Christian sin and still be a Christian? We know Christians sin because 1 John 1:8-9 says if they say they don't, they're liars. John said, "My little children, these things write I unto you, that ye sin not" (1 John 2:1). He wouldn't waste his time writing a letter to Christians about not sinning if Christians never sinned. Christians sin, but they shouldn't. But the question still remains about 1 John 3:6, 9. How can John say we do not sin?

2. Alternative explanations

There have been many explanations of verses 6 and 9. I'll give you six of them.

a) Refers to mortal sins

This explanation comes from Catholic theology, which says a true Christian doesn't commit mortal sins; he only commits venial sins. What's the difference? To the Catholic, a venial sin is not as bad as a mortal sin because the payment for a mortal sin is a person's soul. However, I can't find any basis for that explanation in anything John says. He doesn't say, "Whosoever abides in Him does not commit mortal sins." John says a Christian "sinneth not."

b) Refers to God's overlooking of sin

Some argue that when John says, "Whosoever is born of God doth not commit sin" (v. 9), he means God overlooks our sin. But that's a difficult explanation to hold to if you also believe the Lord chastises those whom He loves for their misbehavior (Heb. 12:3-15). First Corinthians 11:30-32 teaches that certain Christians died because of their sin. Ananias and Sapphira died because of their sin (Acts 5:1-11). If God gets that exercised over sin, you can be sure He regards it in our lives.

c) Refers to the new nature

Some believe 1 John 3:6, 9 mean our new nature can't sin, but our old nature still does. But those verses say nothing about the old and new natures. This argument borrows from Romans 7:17, where the apostle Paul says, "It is no more I that do it, but sin that dwelleth in me." Some interpret this to mean Christians don't sin in the new man; it's the old man that sins (cf. Eph. 4:22-24). I have a difficult time trying to separate the old from the new. I gave up long ago. I do know one thing—when I sin, I'm involved. I cannot detach part of myself and say, "Oops, there goes that old self again!" It isn't that simple. Galatians 2:20 says, "I am crucified with Christ: nevertheless I live." I'm not convinced there are two natures; I think you have one new nature that has the possibility of sinning.

d) Refers to the ideal

Some think John is saying the ideal is that a Christian not sin. But he said, "Whosoever is born of God doth not commit sin" (v. 9). He's making a factual statement, not expressing a wish.

e) Refers to deliberate sin

A popular explanation is that Christians do not commit deliberate sin. John Stott quotes one commentator as saying, "A Christian does not do sin, he suffers it" (*The Epistles of John* [Grand Rapids: Eerdmans, 1980 printing], p. 134). However, I have found that when I sin, I'm usually willfully involved.

f) Refers to habitual sin

I believe this view is the correct one. The best way to find out what John means is to understand the tenses in the Greek text. In verses 6 and 9 John uses the present tense, which expresses habitual, continuous action. Verse 6 literally translates, "Whosoever abides in him does not continually, habitually practice sin." Verse 9 translates, "Whosoever is born of God does not continually, habitually practice sin." Do Christians sin? Sometimes. Do they sin deliberately? Sometimes. But if they are true Christians, they will respond with grief and repentance (Ps. 51). Unsaved people live lives of habitual sin. Even their righteous deeds are filthy rags in God's sight (Isa. 64:6). But Christians do not live lives of habitual sin, and that is the thesis of 1 John 3:4-10.

John gives three reasons illustrating that Christians cannot habitually practice sin. It is incompatible with the law of God, it is incompatible with the work of Christ, and it is incompatible with the ministry of the Holy Spirit.

I. SIN IS INCOMPATIBLE WITH THE LAW OF GOD (v. 4)

"Whosoever [continually, habitually] committeth sin transgresseth also the law; for sin is the transgression of the law."

That translation is not accurate. The text actually says, "Whosoever is continually doing sin is doing lawlessness." The phrase "transgresseth also the law" is the word *anomia* in the Greek text. It means "lawlessness" or "without law." John is not referring to someone who accepts the law and breaks it but to those who live as if there were no law.

A. The Definitions of Sin

There are many definitions of sin in the Bible. Romans 14:23 says, "Whatever is not of faith is sin." To doubt God is sin. James 4:17 says, "To him that knoweth to do good, and doeth it not, to him it is sin." First John 5:17 says, "All unrighteousness is sin." But the best and clearest definition of sin is right here in verse 4: sin is lawlessness. To live as if there were no law is to live as if there were no God. A Christian can't live that way, because Christianity is about living in a relationship with God. John says Christians don't habitually practice sin because that would violate the very nature of God's law.

Don't underestimate sin. Whenever you or I sin, that constitutes open rebellion against God. God has standards. When you became a Christian, He didn't change them or lower them. You still have to obey His moral law, and He gives you the capacity to obey. Sin breaks that law we know so well. It rebels against the God we serve. And it denies that God even exists. Sin is practical atheism, and Christians are anything but atheists. Sin is totally inconsistent with the Christian's life. So John is saying that if certain people claim to be Christians, yet habitually sin, they aren't true believers.

B. The Delight of God's Law

As a Christian, I have submitted to God and His law both lovingly and willingly. My greatest joy is to obey Him and fulfill His will.

1. Scrutinized

   a) Psalm 119

      (1) Verse 1—"Blessed are the undefiled in the way, who walk in the law of the Lord." Characteristic of a believer's manner of life is his obedience to the law of the Lord.

      (2) Verse 34—"Give me understanding, and I shall keep thy law; yea, I shall observe it with my whole heart."

      (3) Verse 44—"So shall I keep thy law continually forever and ever."

      (4) Verse 51—"The proud have had me greatly in derision; yet have I not declined from thy law."

      (5) Verse 55—"I have remembered thy name, O Lord, in the night, and have kept thy law."

      (6) Verse 70—"Their heart is as fat as grease, but I delight in thy law."

      (7) Verse 77—"Let thy tender mercies come unto me, that I may live; for thy law is my delight."

      (8) Verse 92—"Unless thy law had been my delight, I should then have perished in mine affliction."

      (9) Verse 97—"Oh, how love I thy law! It is my meditation all the day."

      (10) Verse 113—"I hate vain thoughts, but thy law do I love."

(11) Verse 163—"I hate and abhor lying, but thy law do I love."

(12) Verse 174—"I have longed for thy salvation, O Lord, and thy law is my delight."

As far back as Old Testament times, it has been characteristic of a believer to love God's law.

b) Romans 6:16-18—"Know ye not that to whom ye yield yourselves servants to obey, his servants ye are whom ye obey" (v. 16). If you've yielded yourself to God, it's obvious that you're going to obey Him. Verses 17-18 say, "God be thanked, that whereas ye were the servants of sin, ye have obeyed from the heart that form of doctrine which was delivered you. Being, then, made free from sin, ye became the servants of righteousness." A Christian is a servant of righteousness, who loves and delights in God's law.

c) Hebrews 8:10—"This is the covenant that I will make with the house of Israel after those days, saith the Lord: I will put my laws into their mind, write them in their hearts." The law of God becomes internal with the New Covenant (cf. Heb. 10:16).

d) Romans 7:15-16, 22-24—Here is a portrait of a Christian who loved the law of God. Verse 15 says, "That which I do I understand not; for what I would, that do I not; but what I hate, that do I." The apostle Paul had a problem: He didn't do the things he should do and wanted to do, but he did what he shouldn't do and didn't want to do. Even though there is the capacity for sin in our new nature as Christians, our desire is to obey the law of God. Verse 16 says, "If, then, I do that which I would not, I consent unto the law that it is good." He loved God's law; He wanted to fulfill it. Verses 22-24 say, "I delight in the law of God after the inward man; but I see another law in my members, warring against the law of my mind, and bringing me into captivity to the law of sin which is in my members. Oh, wretched man that I am!"

That is a picture of a Christian struggling with sin. But what proves to me he is a Christian is his delight in the law of God. Christians are going to sin at times—they're going to do the things they don't want to do and not do the things they want to do. But their delight will be in the law of God. As a result, they will never be characterized by perpetual sin, only occasional sin. The struggle will always be there. The Spirit gave Paul victory. Romans 8:4 says, "The righteousness of the law [will] be fulfilled in us, who walk not after the flesh, but after the Spirit." More than anything else I want to fulfill God's law, but I can't do it on my own. Only the Holy Spirit can do it through me. In Romans 7 Paul shows us how he tried to fulfill the law on his own. In Romans 8 he shows us that we can fulfill the law only through the power of the Holy Spirit. As Christians we are called to fulfill God's law and are empowered to do so.

2. Simplified

 a) Romans 13:8—"He that loveth another hath fulfilled the law." The objective of the Christian life is to obey God and fulfill His will.

 b) Galatians 5:14—"All the law is fulfilled in one word, even in this: Thou shalt love thy neighbor as thyself" (cf. James 2:8). That states the simplicity of fulfilling the law through love.

 c) Galatians 6:2—"Bear ye one another's burdens, and so fulfill the law."

As Christians we love God's law and delight in it. The desire of every believer is to fulfill God's law. If that is not your desire, you are not a Christian. That's not my opinion; that's what the Word of God says. To live as if there were no law and no God contradicts all that Christianity is. We have been saved to be righteous (1 Pet. 2:24; Eph. 2:10). When you were saved, you died to the dominion of sin and were made alive to the dominion of righteousness (Rom. 6). The believer loves God's law. Occasionally he violates it, even willfully, but not persistently and habitually.

In 1 John 3:4 John is telling the assembly that if they want to know who the true believers are, they need only find those who love and obey God's law. The false will stand out because they habitually practice sin. Romans 10:10 says, "With the heart man believeth unto righteousness." First John 2:29 says, "If ye know that he is righteous, ye know that everyone that doeth righteousness is born of him." A true believer is righteous—he obeys the law. The believer and sin are incompatible because sin is incompatible with the law of God.

II. SIN IS INCOMPATIBLE WITH THE WORK OF CHRIST (vv. 5-8)

A. Christ's Removal of Sin (v. 5)

"Ye know that he [Christ] was manifested to take away our sins, and in him is no sin."

To continue in sin is inconsistent with Christ's work because He came to take away our sins. If we did, that would make pointless His death on the cross.

John told the believers that they knew one of the essential facts of Christianity: that God was manifest in the flesh to take away our sins. The Greek word translated "take away" is *airō*, which means "to remove by lifting." The same word is used in John 1:29, where John the Baptist said this regarding Christ: "Behold the Lamb of God, who taketh away the sin of the world." How did Jesus do that? When He died on the cross, He bore our sins in His body. He lifted them off us and took them on Himself.

1. His success

Since it is an indisputable fact that the purpose of Christ's incarnation was to lift sin off us, John says, we therefore would not habitually do that which Christ has removed. Christ didn't say, "I died to remove sins. Unfortunately, it didn't work: people are continuing to habitually sin." Christ *did* remove sin. The minute you were saved, sin stopped being the dominant factor in your life, and righteousness took its place. If that isn't true of you, then you're not a Christian.

a) Ephesians 5:25-27—"Husbands, love your wives, even as Christ also loved the church, and gave himself for it" (v. 25). Why did He give Himself for the church? Verse 26 says, "That he might sanctify and cleanse it . . . that he might present it to himself a glorious church, not having spot, or wrinkle, or any such thing; but that it should be holy and without blemish."

b) Titus 2:14—Christ "gave himself for us, that he might redeem us from all iniquity, and purify unto himself a people of his own, zealous of good works."

Christ came to cleanse us and remove our sin, and that is precisely what He did. Can we habitually do the very thing He came to eliminate? No.

2. His sinlessness

John adds "in him is no sin" to verse 5 just to make sure you don't think that when Christ took your sin, He kept it. Christ is absolutely sinless. As such He was the perfect sacrifice for the sins of others. Second Corinthians 5:21 says, "He hath made him, who knew no sin, to be sin for us, that we might be made the righteousness of God in him." Christians and sin don't mix. Occasionally we sin because we still live in the flesh. But when we were saved, the death of Christ on the cross removed our sin. As a result, we live righteously with occasional sin rather than living sinfully with no occasional righteousness.

B. Christ's Union with Believers (vv. 6-7)

"Whosoever abideth in him sinneth not; whosoever sinneth hath not seen him, neither known him. Little children, let no man deceive you: he that doeth righteousness is righteous, even as he is righteous."

1. The righteousness of believers

If you have been joined to Christ and are abiding in Him, you're not going to sin. You will be righteous like

Him. Our union with Christ means we must exhibit His righteous life.

a) Illustrated

    (1) The resurrection to new life

In Romans 5:20 the apostle Paul says, "Where sin abounded, grace did much more abound." Then he asked this question: "What shall we say then? Shall we continue in sin, that grace may abound? God forbid. How shall we, that are dead to sin, live any longer in it?" (Rom. 6:1-2). As a Christian you can't habitually commit sin because you died to it. Paul then said, "As many of us as were baptized into Jesus Christ were baptized into his death. Therefore, we are buried with him by baptism into death, that as Christ was raised up from the dead by the glory of the Father, even so we also should walk in newness of life. For if we have been planted together in the likeness of his death, we shall also be in the likeness of his resurrection; knowing this, that our old man is crucified with him, that the body of sin might be destroyed, that henceforth we should not serve sin. For he that is dead is freed from sin" (vv. 3-7). Once you have died, sin has done all it can do to you. Romans 6:23 says, "The wages of sin is death." After you died, sin had no claim on you. When did you die? With Christ on the cross. You also rose with Him at His resurrection. Your union with Christ means the death of your old life and the resurrection of your new life.

    (2) The result of new life

Romans 6:11-12 says, "Likewise, reckon ye also yourselves to be dead indeed unto sin, but alive unto God through Jesus Christ, our Lord. Let not sin, therefore, reign in your mortal body." Verse 13 tells us we shouldn't yield our bodies to sin. Then verse 14 says, "For sin shall not have dominion over you." You are now a servant of God; righteousness rules your life. Since we are one with Christ, and He is righteous, the character of our lives is going to be predominantly righteous.

b) Illuminated

When John said, "Whosoever abideth in him sinneth not" (1 John 3:6), he was referring to those who are saved. Whoever is saved does not habitually practice sin. That would be a violation of his union with Christ. It would be ridiculous for Christ to unite sinners to Himself and not do one thing to make them righteous. John also says, "Whosoever sinneth hath not seen him, neither known him" (v. 6). The Greek word translated "know" is *ginōsko*, which means "experiential knowledge." People may claim to be Christians, but if they habitually commit sin, they don't know God.

2. A reminder of the deception

Verse 7 says, "Little children, let no man deceive you." Believers were being deceived, and that was why the letter was written. The Greek word translated "deceive" is *planaō*, which means "to lead astray." The heretics tried to convince the believers that they could sin all they wanted to without harming their spirit. So John replied, "He that doeth righteousness is righteous, even as he [Christ] is righteous" (v. 7).

C. Christ's Destruction of Satan (v. 8)

"He that committeth sin is of the devil; for the devil sinneth from the beginning. For this purpose the Son of God was manifested, that he might destroy the works of the devil."

Someday Christ will destroy the devil himself, but He came primarily to destroy the devil's works. What are the works of the devil? Sin of every kind. Since Christ died on the cross to destroy sin, righteousness has replaced sin in the life of a believer.

1. The source of sin

   John is saying that whoever makes a practice of sin is of
   the devil. The Greek word translated "of" in verse 8 is
   ek, which means "out of." The devil is the source of sin.
   There are only two types of children in this world: the
   children of God and the children of the devil. Those
   who practice righteousness are the children of God;
   those who practice sin are the children of the devil. In
   John 8:44 Jesus tells the Pharisees, "Ye are of your father
   the devil." If you are habitually committing sin, you are
   following the devil. And Jesus came to destroy the
   works of the devil.

2. The scope of destruction

   a) Satan's works

   Satan tempts others to sin, persecutes the church, ac-
   cuses the brethren, sends false teachers, plants evil
   thoughts, enters into people, and rules the world.
   Christ came to destroy those things. The first thing
   He did was to destroy the power of the devil in the
   life of the Christian. First John 4:4 says, "Greater is he
   that is in you, than he that is in the world." Now it
   may seem that Satan is still having his way but not as
   much as he did before we were saved. We are lost
   causes to him.

   The Greek word translated "destroy" is *luō*, which
   means "to loosen," "to undo," or "to remove." Satan's diabolical works were like chains around us.
   When Christ came, He threw off the chains and freed
   us from sin.

   b) Satan's life

   Hebrews 2:14 says, "Forasmuch, then, as the children are partakers of flesh and blood, he also himself
   likewise took part of the same, that through death he
   might destroy him that had the power of death, that
   is, the devil." Christ destroys not only the works of
   the devil but also the devil himself. Revelation 20:2-3,

10, 15 picture the destruction of Satan in the future. Ultimately, Satan will be totally destroyed.

Since Christ came to remove sin, unite us with Himself in His righteousness, and undo the works of the devil, for a believer to habitually practice sin would render the entire work of Christ null and void. The Christian cannot habitually sin because that is incompatible with the law of God and the work of Christ.

III. SIN IS INCOMPATIBLE WITH THE MINISTRY OF THE SPIRIT (v. 9)

"Whosoever is born of God doth not commit sin; for his seed remaineth in him, and he cannot sin, because he is born of God."

A. The Acquisition of the Seed

Salvation involves the acquisition of a seed that remains. When you were saved, the seed of divine life—the life of God Himself—was planted in your life. I became a son of God because I was born of God, and my life is now the life of God. I am now living eternal life, which is a quality of life. Sin can no longer be the habit of such a life.

B. The Work of the Spirit

The Bible teaches that our supernatural birth is the special work of the Holy Spirit. John 3:5 says a man is converted when he is born of the Spirit, whose special work is to generate and regenerate. When God created the heavens and the earth, they were without form and void. Genesis 1:2 says, "The Spirit of God moved upon the face of the waters." The Hebrew word translated "moved" (*rachaph*) is used in Deuteronomy 32:11 to describe an eagle that flutters over her young before she nudges them out of the nest to make them fly. The Spirit of God takes what is there and forces life into it. He broods over it, flutters over it, and generates life into it. As He generated in Genesis, so He regenerates the life of a believer. Second Corinthians 5:17 says, "If any man be in Christ, he is a new creation." That's why I'm not comfortable about the old man/new man concept. You don't keep the old man and have a new man added to it. I don't see this as an addition; I see it as a new life.

1. 1 Peter 1:22-23—"Ye have purified your souls in obeying the truth through the Spirit . . . being born again, not of corruptible seed, but of incorruptible, by the word of God." The Spirit of God uses the Word of God to implant the seed of God.

2. 2 Peter 1:3-4—"His divine power hath given unto us all things that pertain unto life and godliness, through the knowledge of him that hath called us to glory and virtue; by which are given unto us exceedingly great and precious promises, that by these ye might be partakers of the divine nature."

Since believers have a new life, they cannot habitually sin because they are born of God. We are all new creatures.

Conclusion

In 1 John 3:10 John sums up his thoughts: "In this the children of God are manifest, and the children of the devil: whosoever doeth not righteousness is not of God, neither he that loveth not his brother." I don't care what anyone claims—if people are not righteous, they are not Christians. A Christian habitually practices righteousness but occasionally sins; he doesn't habitually sin but occasionally practice "righteousness."

Sin is incompatible with the law of God, the work of Christ, and the ministry of the Holy Spirit. When I think about that, sin in my life becomes all the more rotten. Even occasional sin isn't right. In the 1940s a famous newspaper, the *London Daily Mail,* strove to be error-free. The management offered rewards for finding errors and even fired employees who made errors. Nothing worked. Finally they found the perfect solution: they printed the first copy of the press run on expensive paper for the king of England. The errors dropped 90 percent. Similarly, your life and my life are to be lived for the King. We must live our lives as near to perfection as we can.

Focusing on the Facts

1. What two parts of John's moral test are in 1 John 3:10 (see p. 49)?
2. What did the Gnostics believe about sin (see p. 49)?
3. What are the two critical statements in 1 John 3:4-10? Why are they critical (see p. 50)?
4. What are the six explanations offered for the meaning of those two critical statements? Which is best and why (see pp. 50-52)?
5. Why are Christians unable to habitually practice sin (see p. 52)?
6. What is the meaning of *anomia* as John uses it in 1 John 3:4 (see p. 53)?
7. Give some definitions of sin (see p. 53).
8. What should be the greatest joy for a Christian? Cite some verses that express that joy (see pp. 54-55).
9. What simplifies fulfilling the law (see p. 56)?
10. What is one of the essential facts of Christianity (see 1 John 3:5)? What effect does that have on the believer's behavior (see pp. 57-58)?
11. Why was Christ the perfect sacrifice (1 John 3:5; see p. 58)?
12. What kind of life will the believer live as a result of his union with Christ (see pp. 58-59)?
13. What reminder did John issue to believers in 1 John 3:7 (see p. 60)?
14. What are the works of the devil (see p. 60)?
15. What is the source of those who habitually practice sin (see p. 61)?
16. When people are saved, what is planted in them? What is the result (see p. 62)?

Pondering the Principles

1. Is there any habitual sin in your life? Examine carefully your walk with God. Isolate occasional sin from any sin you find has become repetitive. Why has this sin become a habit? Do you really want to eliminate this sin from your life? Are you taking it seriously enough? You need to make a commitment to say no to sin. Ask God for guidance in eliminating habitual sin.

2. How much do you delight in God's law? What actions on your part manifest your love for God's law? Can unbelievers see your

joy in God's Word through those actions? If not, what changes in attitude do you need to make that will result in right actions?

3. If you are a believer, Christ has removed your sin, united you with Himself, and destroyed the works of Satan. How should that affect the way you live? Do you live as if those facts are true? Read 1 John 3:5-8. Meditate on those verses. Thank Christ for His work on your behalf.

4
How's Your Love Life?

Outline

Introduction
A. The Mark of a Christian
B. The Message of Love

Lesson
I. The Children of the Devil (vv. 11-17)
  A. Murder (vv. 11-12)
    1. The character of Abel
       a) Abel and the religion of grace
       b) Cain and the religion of human achievement
    2. The character of Cain
       a) He was a child of Satan
       b) He perverted God's worship
       c) He was jealous of Abel
  B. Hate (vv. 13-15)
    1. The attitude of the world (v. 13)
    2. The assurance of believers (v. 14)
    3. The analysis of hate (v. 15)
       a) Proverbs 6:17
       b) Matthew 5:21-22
  C. Indifference (vv. 16-17)
    1. The definition of love
    2. The deeds of love
       a) Implemented
       b) Illustrated
II. The Children of God (vv. 18-24)
  A. Their Character (v. 18)
  B. Their Blessings (vv. 19-24)

1. Assurance (vv. 19-20)
   a) Pacifying the conscience (v. 19)
   b) Purging the conscience (v. 20)
      (1) Condemnation from the conscience
      (2) Commendation from God
         (*a*) Appealing to God's knowledge
         (*b*) Amplifying God's knowledge
2. Answered prayer (vv. 21-22)
   a) Confidence toward God
   b) Conditions of answered prayer
      (1) No unconfessed sin
      (2) Obedience to the Word
      (3) Doing what pleases God
3. Abiding (vv. 23-24)

Conclusion

Introduction

A commercial some years ago asked this important question: How's your love life? Apparently enough people are concerned about their love life to make advertisers on Madison Avenue think it's a good way to promote their product. I can't help but think that John is asking the same question in this text. He uses it to monitor the legitimacy of those who claim to be Christians, because true Christians love one another. One of the key tests of Christianity is love.

According to 1 John 2 the believer will love God and others but will not love the world. In 1 John 3 Christians are referred to as the children of God. Two things mark the child of God: righteousness and love. Righteousness is the theme of verses 4-10 (see pp. 48-63); love is the theme of verses 11-24. Verse 10 acts as the transition.

A. The Mark of a Christian

Love for our brothers and sisters in Christ is an indispensable mark of a Christian. Romans 5:5 says, "The love of God is shed abroad in our hearts." And the love God puts in our hearts will transmit itself to others. Paul told the Thessalonians, "Ye need not that I write unto you; for ye yourselves are taught of God to love one another" (1 Thess.

4:9). There will be occasions when we will not love one another, but the habit of our lives will be to love one another.

B. The Message of Love

First John 3:11 says, "This is the message that ye heard from the beginning, that we should love one another." That is not merely a duty; it is proof of true Christianity. The heretics boasted of their union with God and their knowledge of the truth, but they had no love for the believers. They separated themselves and lorded their will over them. They had no community spirit.

"The message that ye heard from the beginning" refers to the teaching of the apostles. It has always been the same: believers should love one another. The heretics, particularly the gnostic heretics, boasted about new teaching. That's why John repeatedly referred back to apostolic authority, which is foundational and unchanging (1 John 1:1, 5; 2:24). Many new doctrines have come and gone. Christians are to reject new doctrines and hold fast to the truth of Scripture.

Truth does not change. And truth regarding Christian conduct is just as unalterable as truth of Christ. A person who claims to be a Christian but does not habitually practice righteousness and love is no Christian at all. When you become a Christian you are no longer totally dominated by sin; you tend to do righteous things (although there will be occasional sin). You also begin to love your brothers and sisters in Christ.

The Circular Epistle

Some commentators have likened 1 John to a spiral that gets larger and larger. John repeats the same arguments, only each time it encompasses more territory. John discusses righteousness and love in 1 John 5 but in different ways than he does in chapter 3.

A teacher needs to remember two things about his students: forgetfulness and familiarity. Whatever they are taught, they will forget. A teacher should repeat himself. But if he says the same thing in the same way, the students won't listen. So a good teacher should teach the same thing in a different way so his pupils can't tell. Peter told his readers he would not cease to help them remember (2 Pet. 1:15). Whenever we hear a familiar truth presented in a different way, we get excited about it. John repeats himself but never in the same way.

In 1 John 3:11-24 John discusses love. First he characterizes the children of the devil; then he characterizes the children of God.

Lesson

I. THE CHILDREN OF THE DEVIL (vv. 11-17)

Jesus told the Pharisees, "Ye are of your father the devil" (John 8:44). The devil's children are all who don't know Jesus Christ. Let's examine three characteristics of the children of the devil as they relate to love.

A. Murder (vv. 11-12)

"This is the message that ye heard from the beginning, that we should love one another. Not as Cain, who was of that wicked one, and killed his brother." Genesis 4 tells us about Cain and his brother Abel. Verses 1-2 say, "Adam knew Eve his wife; and she conceived, and bore Cain, and said, I have gotten a man from the Lord. And she again bore his brother, Abel. And Abel was a keeper of sheep, but Cain was a tiller of the ground."

1. The character of Abel

    a) Abel and the religion of grace

    Verse 3 says, "In process of time it came to pass, that Cain brought of the fruit of the ground an offering unto the Lord." That was an act of worship. Verses 4-5 say, "Abel, he also brought of the firstlings of his flock and of the fat thereof. And the Lord had respect unto Abel and to his offering; but unto Cain and to his offering he had not respect." It's obvious from the context that God had already revealed to them that a

70

blood sacrifice was the only acceptable sacrifice (cf. Gen. 3:21). Hebrews 9:22 says, "Without shedding of blood there is no remission [of sins]." God instituted blood sacrifices as the only proper form of worship, and Abel obeyed.

b) Cain and the religion of human achievement

Cain brought God the fruit of the ground—that which he himself had planted and harvested. He offered what he wanted to offer, not what God wanted him to offer. He invented his own religion, and the Lord would have none of it. Genesis 4:5-7 says, "Cain was very angry, and his countenance fell. And the Lord said unto Cain, Why art thou angry? And why is thy countenance fallen? If thou doest well, shalt thou not be accepted? And if thou doest not well, sin lieth at the door."

Verse 8 says, "Cain talked with Abel his brother: and it came to pass, when they were in the field, that Cain rose up against Abel, his brother, and slew him." He murdered him. First John 3:12 says Cain murdered Abel "because his own works were evil, and his brother's righteous." Cain was jealous of Abel.

2. The character of Cain

a) He was a child of Satan

Cain "was of that wicked one" (v. 12). The Greek word translated "wicked one" is *ponēros*. It is stronger than *kakos*, the usual Greek word for evil. *Ponēros* speaks of evil in active opposition to good—organized evil. A man who is *kakos* is willing to be evil and perish in his own corruption, but the person who is *ponēros* seeks to drag everyone else down with him. Who is the evil one? Satan. Cain was a child of Satan. That is made evident because he was a murderer. God's children are not murderers; they love one another. John 8:44 says Satan has been a murderer from the beginning.

b) He perverted God's worship

The Greek word translated "killed" in 1 John 3:12 is *sphazō*, which means "to butcher by cutting the throat." It is used in the Septuagint (the Greek version of the Old Testament) to refer to the slaying of animals for Levitical sacrifices. It is quite probable that Cain cut Abel's throat. When Cain and Abel were born, the seeds of death had already been implanted in the sins of Adam and Eve. But as far as we know, no one had yet died. That Cain knew how to kill implies he knew God required an animal sacrifice. God instituted a pattern of sacrifice to bring men to Himself, but Cain became the first to pervert it and turn it into murder. The human race learned to murder when it was taught to worship.

c) He was jealous of Abel

Why did Cain kill his brother? Verse 12 says, "Because his own works were evil, and his brother's righteous." He was jealous—his brother was accepted by God, but he wasn't. Jealousy lay at the base of Cain's murder. That's what life is like for the children of the devil.

Not all people are murderers as Cain was, and that leads to the next characteristic of a child of the devil.

B. Hate (vv. 13-15)

1. The attitude of the world (v. 13)

"Marvel not [stop marveling], my brethren, if the world hate you."

Don't be surprised if the world hates you. Most people have never murdered anyone, but the only difference between hate and murder is the act—the attitude is the same. There are a lot of haters in this world who don't murder for one reason—fear of the consequences. If they could get away with it without punishment, guilt, and negative social reaction, they would. In God's eyes, hatred is the moral equivalent of murder.

We could translate verse 13 this way: "Since the world hates you, don't be shocked." Cain was the prototype of the world; he manifested the ugly qualities Satan generates in every one of his children. The hatred the world has for righteousness began with Cain and has perpetuated itself since then. Believers shouldn't be surprised by that. We expect the devil to hate God; likewise we can expect the children of the devil to hate the children of God. You may think they don't hate you, but they do. I'm not saying everyone in the world is horrible and can't love, but the general pattern of godless people is murder and hatred. The wicked system will continue to hate believers.

2. The assurance of believers (v. 14)

"We know that we have passed from death unto life, because we love the brethren. He that loveth not his brother abideth in death."

If you have ever doubted your salvation, you can take comfort in this verse. You can know you have passed from death to life if you have a continuous and habitual love for Christians. The world doesn't love Christians. Dead people don't love; only living people do. Love is the surest test of divine life. Where there is no love, there is spiritual death. Examine your heart. Do you love other Christians? Do you seek the fellowship of Christians? If you do, you have passed from death to life. If you do not, you're still dead.

3. The analysis of hate (v. 15)

"Whosoever hateth his brother is a murderer; and ye know that no murderer hath eternal life abiding in him."

Hatred is the same as murder in the eyes of God. And murderers do not have eternal life. As a general pattern, a believer loves, and an unbeliever hates.

a) Proverbs 6:17—The Lord hates "a proud look, a lying tongue, and hands that shed innocent blood." The Lord hates murderous hands. God's children do not commit murder. According to 1 John 3:15 one who hates is guilty of murder. In God's eyes the ethic is the same.

    b) Matthew 5:21-22—In the Sermon on the Mount Jesus says, "Ye have heard that it was said by them of old, Thou shalt not kill and whosoever shall kill shall be in danger of judgment; but I say unto you that whosoever is angry with his brother without a cause shall be in danger of judgment; and whosoever shall say to his brother, Raca, shall be in danger of the council; but whosoever shall say, Thou fool, shall be in danger of hell fire." The attitude you have toward your brother is as significant to Jesus as what you do to him.

There are few people who murder as a way of life, but there are many who hate others.

C. Indifference (vv. 16-17)

"By this perceive we the love of God, because he laid down his life for us; and we ought to lay down our lives for the brethren. But whosoever hath this world's good, and seeth his brother have need, and shutteth up his compassions from him, how dwelleth the love of God in him?"

A person who sees a Christian in need and has the ability to help, yet refuses to do so, is not a Christian according to John. The world is characterized by indifference and apathy. The world murders its own, but Christians care for each other with sacrificial love.

1. The definition of love

Love is not defined as an attitude or an emotion but as an act of self-sacrifice. We know God loves us because He laid down His life for us. What should we do? Lay down our lives for the brethren. Cain hated and murdered his brother—that's how Satan's children behave. Christ gave up His life for those He loved. First Peter 2:21 says, "Christ also suffered for us, leaving us an example."

2. The deeds of love

Chances are you won't have the opportunity to die for someone, and that's why John added verse 17: "Whosoever hath this world's good, and seeth his brother have need, and shutteth up his compassions from him, how dwelleth the love of God in him?" True love isn't confined to dying for someone. A Christian is willing to surrender possessions, comfort, and anything of value if a fellow brother has need.

a) Implemented

Verse 17 says, "Whosoever hath this world's good, and seeth his *brother*" (emphasis added). Christians are especially to meet the needs of their brothers in Christ. John is not teaching us to give out money and resources to all people indiscriminately. You can pacify yourself by doing so, but you'll never become close to anyone. You should be meeting needs within the community of believers. Certainly you can meet needs outside that community as God brings people across your path.

b) Illustrated

Luke 10:30-31 says, "A certain man went down from Jerusalem to Jericho, and fell among thieves, who stripped him of his raiment, and wounded him, and departed, leaving him half dead. And by chance there came down a certain priest that way; and when he saw him, he passed by on the other side." The priest proved he was a child of the devil because he ignored the man lying in the road half dead. He didn't want to defile himself. Jesus continued the narrative: "Likewise a Levite, when he was at the place, came and looked on him, and passed by on the other side. But a certain Samaritan, as he journeyed, came where he was; and when he saw him, he had compassion on him, and went to him, and bound up his wounds, pouring in oil and wine, and set him on his own beast, and brought him to an inn, and took care of him. And on the next day, when he departed, he took out two denarii, and gave them to the host, and said unto him, Take care of him; and whatever thou spendest more, when I come again, I will repay thee. Which, now, of these three, thinkest thou, was neighbor unto him that fell among the thieves?" (vv. 32-36).

Two acted as children of the devil; one acted as a child of God by showing love to the victim. All three were responsible to help—they all recognized the man's need, and they had what he needed. If we're not willing to give, then John questions our salvation.

Verse 17 uses the phrase "shutteth up his compassions [KJV, "bowels"]." The Greek word used here refers to the heart. The Jews spoke of the seat of a man's emotions as the bowels—we say it's the heart. Actually, it's neither place. They serve merely as a physical identification. A man who shuts up his bowels has turned off his compassion.

If you are habitually uncaring and indifferent, John questions your salvation. If you murder, hate, and are indifferent, you have no eternal life abiding in you.

The High Risk of Christian Service

1. Sacrifice means risk

Children of God make supreme sacrifices for one another. In Philippians 2:26-27 Paul says about Epaphroditus: "He longed after you all, and was full of heaviness, because ye had heard that he had been sick. For, indeed, he was sick near unto death, but God had mercy on him; and not on him only, but on me also, lest I should have sorrow upon sorrow." Verse 30 tells us how he became so sick: "For the work of Christ, he was near unto death, not regarding his life."

Do you risk anything in your Christian life, or do you measure it out carefully? If so, you haven't learned to make a sacrifice as Epaphroditus did. He was willing to pay the price of death. Paul told the Philippians, "If I be offered upon the sacrifice and service of your faith, I joy" (Phil. 2:17). He was ready to die if that was necessary for their salvation. We don't fully understand that kind of sacrifice. But we do know something about it if we are true Christians. We are to love the way Jesus loved.

2. Sacrifice means sharing

Christians share. That's part of what the Christian life is all about.

a) 1 Timothy 6:17—"Charge them that are rich in this age, that they be not high-minded, nor trust in uncertain riches but in the living God, who giveth us richly all things to enjoy; that they do good, that they be rich in good works, ready to distribute, willing to share."

b) Hebrews 13:16—"Do good and to share forget not; for with such sacrifices God is well pleased."

In 1 John 3:11-17 John describes the children of the devil. They murder, hate, and are indifferent.

II. THE CHILDREN OF GOD (vv. 18-24)

The children of God are characterized by love, which originates in God, issues in self-sacrifice, and is evidence of eternal life.

A. Their Character (v. 18)

"My little children, let us not love in word, neither in tongue, but in deed and in truth."

Our love is to be in action, not in word. Profession is not enough; action is essential. What does John mean when he says, "Let us not love in word"? He is referring to all talk and no action. What does he mean when he says, "Let us not love . . . in tongue"? That implies hypocrisy. Don't let your love be all talk and no action, and don't let it be hypocritical. You need to love in deed and in truth—in action and in honesty.

B. Their Blessings (vv. 19-24)

   1. Assurance (vv. 19-20)

      a) Pacifying the conscience (v. 19)

"By this we know that we are of the truth, and shall assure our hearts before him."

How can we assure our hearts? By loving in deed and in truth. When you can pinpoint deeds of self-sacrifice in your life, you can eliminate doubts and insecurity. The children of the devil don't love Christians. Our hearts will experience uncertainty, insecurity, and self-condemnation. But the remedy for that is loving in deed and in truth. And the fruit of love is assurance.

The Greek word translated "assure" is *peithō*, which means "to persuade" or "to tranquilize." If your heart is upset, tranquilize it by reminding it of your deeds of love. No unsaved person can have that kind of assurance.

      b) Purging the conscience (v. 20)

"If our heart condemn us, God is greater than our heart, and knoweth all things."

        (1) Condemnation from the conscience

Sometimes your heart will condemn you. Mine does. Sometimes it's right; sometimes it's wrong. I can condemn myself for wrong things. I expect things out of myself that the Lord doesn't expect. I can have certain legalistic quirks. Sometimes I get lazy. Sometimes after I've been working on a message for six or seven hours I'm ready to quit and do nothing. For a couple of hours my conscience tells me that I'm a sluggard. In some cases, my conscience is wrong—there are times I am tired and need the rest—but in other cases my conscience is right. When your conscience is wrong, reject it; when it's right, confess the sin.

(2) Commendation from God

If your conscience condemns you, remember that God is greater than your heart and knows all things (v. 20). God doesn't condemn you. Romans 8:1 says, "There is . . . no condemnation to them who are in Christ Jesus." The next time your conscience condemns you, remember that it isn't God who is condemning you. You may think God doesn't know you as you know yourself, but He is greater than your heart and knows all things. When your conscience starts to condemn you, remember the pattern of love for the brethren you have exhibited. God will confirm that you stand uncondemned.

A condemning conscience robs a believer of assurance. When you concentrate on the failures of your life, your conscience will tear down your assurance. You must remember that it has been characteristic of you to make sacrifices for other Christians. God, who knows you, is greater than your heart and doesn't want to condemn you; He wants to assure you.

(a) Appealing to God's knowledge

In John 21:17 Jesus says to Peter, "Lovest thou me?" Peter replied, "Lord, thou knowest all things; thou knowest that I love thee." He appealed to the Lord's omniscience. As a Christian, I assure my heart by my deeds of love. I can appeal to God because He is greater than my conscience. Don't let your conscience rob you of joy. Don't let it rob you of your security and confidence. God doesn't condemn your heart; why should you condemn yourself?

(b) Amplifying God's knowledge

God knows that the worst that is in the Christian is superficial. He looks down on the deep things and sees the truth. In Romans 7:22 Paul says, "I delight in the law of God after the inward man." God sees the deep reality. Black deeds may rise to the surface to condemn us, but God sees true love deep in our hearts, which is revealed by our deeds of self-sacrifice. I may commit a sin, but God isn't going to condemn me for that sin. He knows I'm His child. The pattern of my life has been characterized by godliness and sacrificial love. When I sin, that is not the real me. Romans 7:17 says, "It is no more I that do it, but sin that dwelleth in me." I'm not telling you to take sin lightly—God doesn't. He will discipline you for it (Heb. 12:6). But know He will forgive your sin and won't condemn you for it.

2. Answered prayer (vv. 21-22)

"Beloved, if our heart condemn us not, then have we confidence toward God. And whatever we ask, we receive of him, because we keep his commandments, and do those things that are pleasing in his sight."

a) Confidence toward God

Love banishes self-condemnation. When I recognize the deeds of love I have done, my insecurity is gone. If you're still condemning yourself with artificial guilt, then you're playing God. You are saying that you are a higher authority than He is. If you will accept the fact He doesn't condemn you, if you will confess your sin and turn from it, and if you will recognize the deeds of love in your life, your heart won't condemn you. Instead, you'll have confidence in God. And you will receive what you ask.

b) Conditions of answered prayer

There are three conditions for answered prayer.

(1) No unconfessed sin

Psalm 66:18 says, "If I regard iniquity in my heart, the Lord will not hear me." According to

1 John 3:21, when you confess your sin, your heart will no longer condemn you.

(2) Obedience to the Word

Verse 22 says, "Whatever we ask, we receive of him, because we keep [obey] his commandments." First Peter 3:7 says a husband and wife won't have their prayers answered unless they are obedient.

(3) Doing what pleases God

Verse 22 says, "Because we keep his commandments, and do those things that are pleasing in his sight."

James says most people pray for things to satisfy their lusts (James 4:3). The habitual behavior of a Christian is love, obedience, and doing what pleases God. As a result, his prayers are answered. Love characterizes God's children and results in assurance and answered prayer.

3. Abiding (vv. 23-24)

"And this is his commandment, that we should believe on the name of his Son, Jesus Christ, and love one another, as he gave us commandment. And he that keepeth his commandments dwelleth in him, and he in him. And by this we know that he abideth in us, by the Spirit whom he hath given us."

According to verse 22 the believer believes, obeys, and loves. The result is that we dwell "in him, and he in [us]. And by this we know that he abideth in us, by the Spirit whom he hath given us" (v. 24). The third great blessing of the children of God is the abiding presence of the Holy Spirit.

Conclusion

The children of the devil are characterized by an unloving heart full of murder, hate, and indifference. The children of God are characterized by love, which results in assurance, answered prayer, and knowledge through the Holy Spirit that we abide in Him and He in us. The proof that you are a Christian is simple: Do you believe in the Lord Jesus Christ? Do you love the brothers? Do you obey His commandments?

Focusing on the Facts

1. What is an indispensable mark of a Christian (see p. 68)?
2. Why did John continually refer back to apostolic authority (see p. 69)?
3. Explain how 1 John can be likened to a spiral (see pp. 69-70).
4. Why did God favor Abel's offering and not Cain's (see pp. 70-71)?
5. Why did Cain murder Abel (1 John 3:12; see p. 71)?
6. Define the Greek word translated "wicked" in 1 John 3:12 (see p. 71).
7. Explain how Cain knew how to murder Abel (see p. 72).
8. What is the only difference between hate and murder (see p. 72)?
9. According to 1 John 3:14, how can believers be assured of their salvation (see p. 73)?
10. Define love. What should a believer be willing to do (see pp. 74-75)?
11. In the parable of the Good Samaritan (Luke 10:30-36), why were the priest, Levite, and Samaritan each responsible to help the victim (see p. 76)?
12. Explain what "shutteth up his compassions [or "bowels"]" means (1 John 3:17; see p. 76).
13. What did Epaphroditus risk and why (Phil. 2:26-30; see pp. 76-77)?
14. What does "let us not love in word, neither in tongue" mean (1 John 3:18; see p. 77)?
15. How can a Christian eliminate doubt and insecurity in his life (see p. 78)?
16. What does a condemning conscience steal from the believer (see p. 78)?

17. Why can the Christian appeal to God when his conscience starts to condemn him (see p. 79)?

18. What are the three conditions to answered prayer? Explain each (see pp. 80-81).

Pondering the Principles

1. Cain killed Abel because he was jealous of him. Are you jealous of a brother or sister in Christ? Why? Is it his or her job, position in the church, ministry, possessions, or level of spiritual growth? Isolate the specific problem. Confess any hatred that has built up inside you as a result of your jealousy. Ask God to replace that hatred with active love toward that brother or sister. Start today with deeds of kindness.

2. The apostle John tells us we shouldn't be shocked that the world hates Christians. Why? What things have you done to cause a negative reaction from unbelievers? How did the Lord use that situation to reveal His glory? Have you failed to confront ungodly people with the gospel when given the opportunity? If you see that area as an ongoing weakness, reevaluate your priorities. Make sure witnessing to unbelievers has its proper place along with all the other aspects of your Christian walk.

3. How would you describe your prayer life? If it seems as though God isn't responding, perhaps you aren't meeting the conditions for answered prayer (see pp. 80-81). Review them. Which of the three is a weakness in your life? If it's unconfessed sin, examine yourself and confess any sin you find. If you are being disobedient to God, confess that. Increase the time you spend in reading and studying God's Word so that you will be more sensitive to times of disobedience. If you are not doing things that are pleasing to God, begin to view God more as your Father. Just as a small child wants to please his human father, seek to please your heavenly Father.

5
Test the Spirits

Outline

Introduction
A. The Significance of False Doctrine
    1. Essentials of false doctrine
       a) Doubt
       b) Distortion
       c) Denial
       d) Deceit
    2. Examples of biblical warnings
B. The Source of False Doctrine
    1. Demonic activity
       a) Seductive spirits
       b) Sacrificial worship
          (1) 1 Corinthians 10:19-22
          (2) Deuteronomy 32:17
          (3) Psalm 106:36-37
       c) Symbolic language
          (1) Their appearance
          (2) Their deception
    2. Deceptive operations
       a) Through human agents
          (1) Acts 20:30-31
          (2) 2 Peter 2:1
       b) Through human systems

Lesson
I. The Command (v. 1*a*)
A. Stop Believing
B. Start Testing

Introduction

A. The Significance of False Doctrine

The Bible is full of warnings against error and the corruption of God's revelation. Satan and his demons are busy corrupting God's truth, propagating worldwide error, and confusing people. According to 2 Corinthians 11:14-15, Satan appears as an angel of light and his demons as ministers of righteousness. They mask themselves as those who give God's truth when in fact they give the opposite.

1. Essentials of false doctrine

False doctrine has been the great plague of the earth throughout the history of man. It began in the Garden of Eden: the first temptation was based on an effort to corrupt the word of God.

a) Doubt

Satan said to Eve, "Hath God said?" (Gen. 3:1), planting doubt in her mind.

b) Distortion

Eve replied that God had said, "Ye shall not eat of it, neither shall ye touch it" (Gen. 3:3). But God hadn't said anything about not touching the tree.

c) Denial

Satan told Eve, "Ye shall not surely die" (Gen. 3:4), a direct contradiction of what God said previously (Gen. 2:17).

d) Deceit

Satan is busy deceiving people about what is true. His demons wage a persistent and endless counter-campaign to keep men ignorant of divinely revealed truth and salvation.

2. Examples of biblical warnings

a) Moses passionately exhorted the Israelites to serve the Lord and not to forget His precepts (Deut. 9).

b) David gave the same counsel to Israel and to his son Solomon (1 Chron. 28).

c) The prophets warned the people not to compromise their commitment to the Word of God.

d) The Lord Jesus Christ predicted the coming of false prophets and false christs (Matt. 24:5, 11).

e) The apostle Paul cautioned the Ephesian elders about the coming of grievous wolves who would not spare the flock and would speak perverse things (Acts 20:29-30).

f) The apostle Peter warned about apostates who would teach false doctrine (2 Pet. 2).

False doctrine is a problem we face constantly. We are confronted with differing opinions that constitute the false doctrine of Satan's deception.

B. The Source of False Doctrine

Although the Bible primarily focuses on the human agents propagating false doctrine, it also deals with the source of false doctrine: Satan and his demons.

1. Demonic activity

Behind all false teachers are invisible demons. No false teacher teaches from his own wisdom; a demon or demons inspire him to teach. False teachers are mouthpieces for Satan.

a) Seductive spirits

First Timothy 4:1 says, "The Spirit speaketh expressly that, in the latter times, some shall depart from the faith, giving heed to seducing spirits." Most of us don't talk to seducing spirits, but you've heard their propaganda coming out of false prophets, their mouthpieces. The doctrines they teach are not those of distorted men; they are the doctrines of demons (1 Tim. 4:1).

First Timothy 4:1 emphatically links false doctrine with demonism. False teachers and false prophets are not primarily to blame for false doctrine; demons deserve the blame. The man is only the mouthpiece. The next time you hear someone propagating something contrary to Scripture, you can be sure it's demon influenced.

Doctrines of demons have been propagated since Genesis 4. The first came through Cain. He believed he could worship God in any way he liked. That was the first false doctrine and is probably the most popular one. Demonic religions teach salvation by works.

All systems apart from the truth are demonic, even those masquerading as Christianity.

b) Sacrificial worship

(1) 1 Corinthians 10:19-22—Paul said, "What say I, then? That the idol is anything?" (v. 19). If someone wants to worship an idol, he is worshiping nothing, because an idol is nothing. However, the idol in reality is something it isn't supposed to be. In verse 20 Paul says, "But I say that the things which the Gentiles sacrifice, they sacrifice to demons." What they think is an idol is really a demon. I used to wonder how someone could worship a rock all his life, and how generation after generation could worship the same rock. Perhaps the demon impersonating the god they think is in the rock does enough to keep them worshiping it.

Verses 20-22 then add, "I would not that ye should have fellowship with demons. Ye cannot drink the cup of the Lord, and the cup of demons; ye cannot be partakers of the Lord's table, and of the table of demons. Do we provoke the Lord to jealousy? Are we stronger than he?" While an idol is nothing at all, there is a terrible reality underlying that idol: a demon or demons impersonating the god supposedly in the idol.

(2) Deuteronomy 32:17—"They sacrificed unto demons, not to God." When the people sacrificed to their idols, they were actually sacrificing to demons.

(3) Psalm 106:36-37—"They served their idols, which were a snare unto them. Yea, they sacrificed their sons and their daughters unto demons."

A person who worships an idol or even something more sophisticated is actually worshiping demons. Supernatural things will occur to hold him to that system. The demons will manifest enough of the supernatural to maintain their facade.

c) Symbolic language

There is much symbolic language in the book of Revelation. Symbolism is used to give a spiritual reality understanding and meaning in human terms. Demons are seen as many different symbols. One of those symbols is frogs.

(1) Their appearance

Revelation 16:13 says, "I saw three unclean spirits, like frogs, come out of the mouth of the dragon [Satan], and out of the mouth of the beast [the Antichrist], and out of the mouth of the false prophet." The satanic trinity will spawn those demons. Verse 14 clarifies that they are demons: "They are the spirits of demons, working miracles, that go forth unto the kings of the earth and of the whole world, to gather them to the battle of that great day of God Almighty." Verse 16 says they gather them together at Armageddon.

(2) Their deception

Those froglike demons will deceive the entire world, tricking the kings of the world into gathering at Armageddon to do what the demons want them to do. The world thinks it's going to do one thing, but the demons have another plan—preventing Jesus Christ from setting up His kingdom on earth.

2. Deceptive operations

   a) Through human agents

Demons usually operate through human agents. Satan and his demons use many different approaches. They may use atheism, Communism, animism, polytheism, or some form of idolatry. Of particular importance is their deceptive efforts within the context of Christianity. They are active within the faith doing all they can to destroy it.

(1) Acts 20:30-31—Paul said, *"Of your own selves* shall men arise, speaking perverse things, to draw away disciples after them. . . . For the space of three years I ceased not to warn everyone night and day with tears" (emphasis added).

(2) 2 Peter 2:1—"There were false prophets also *among the people,* even as there shall be false teachers among you, who secretly shall bring in destructive heresies" (emphasis added). The biggest problem comes from the inside.

b) Through human systems

Demonic deception leaves no doctrine unattacked. In New Testament times they used legalism, antinomianism, and Gnosticism. Two thousand years later, all those initial deceptions have developed into elaborate systems such as Spiritism, Theosophy, Christian Science, Mormonism, Jehovah's Witnesses, Unitarianism, Liberalism, and Modernism. All contain satanic deceptions and doctrines of demons.

The Gnostics propagated the teaching that Jesus wasn't the Christ—God incarnate. John was concerned because they were confusing the believers. He wrote 1 John to unmask those false teachers. In chapter 4 John informs us of the demons behind the false teachers. He applies the doctrinal test: do the false teachers believe in Christ? He wants to show the believers how to distinguish a demon spirit from the Holy Spirit. First John 4 begins with the command to test, the need to test, the method of the test, and the application of the test.

Lesson

I. THE COMMAND (v. 1*a*)

"Beloved, believe not every spirit, but test the spirits whether they are of God."

The reason to test the spirits is that "many false prophets are gone out into the world" (v. 1). In verse 1 John links false prophets with demons. When a teacher opens his mouth, he represents either the spirit of truth or the spirit of error (v. 6). The spirit of truth is the Holy Spirit, and the spirit of error is a demon.

A. Stop Believing

The word *beloved* in verse 1 has to refer to Christians, because unbelievers have no hope of knowing how to evaluate truth or test the spirits. First John 3:24 says, "By this we know that he abideth in us, by the Spirit whom he hath given us." Believers have the Holy Spirit, but there are other spirits in the world. They need to be careful to find out if a certain teaching is from the Holy Spirit or some other spirit. John tells us to stop believing every spirit in 1 John 4:1. He is forbidding continuation of an action already occurring.

People will sometimes bring into the assembly of believers a teaching that is totally without basis and announce it as God's truth. If that happens, don't believe it. Guard against deceptive spirits. Don't believe everything you hear and read.

B. Start Testing

In verse 1 John says, "Test the spirits whether they are of God." The Greek word translated "test" is *dokimazō*, a term for testing people in high office. The verb is in the present tense—the believer is to continually test the spirits.

II. THE REASON (v. 1b)

"Many false prophets are gone out into the world."

A. The Proliferation of False Prophets

We will be deceived if we don't test the spirits, because there are so many of them. They come from the spirit of error. A good series of verses to memorize is 1 Thessalonians 5:16-21, and verse 21 applies especially to 1 John 4:1,

"Prove [test] all things; hold fast that which is good."
Verse 20 says not to despise prophesying. We're to put it to
the test and hang onto it if it's good. Satan is both clever
and subtle, so you have to be careful.

B. The Prophecies of False Prophets

    1. Matthew 7:15—"Beware of false prophets, who come to
       you in sheep's clothing, but inwardly they are ravening
       wolves." They won't announce who they are; they will
       mask themselves and appear to be moved by the Holy
       Spirit.

    2. Mark 13:22-23—"False Christs [Gk., *pseudo christoi*] and
       false prophets shall rise, and shall show signs and
       wonders, to seduce, if it were possible, even the elect"
       (v. 22). Is it possible to seduce the elect? Ultimately, no.
       But deceivers will try. Verse 23 says, "Take heed; be-
       hold, I have foretold you all things." There are many
       voices in this world. Go into a Christian bookstore, and
       look at what's on the shelves. There's a lot of material,
       and it's hard to know what's good and what's not.
       There are many people talking on the radio and preach-
       ing in churches. A lot of them ask for your money.
       Many Christians are gullible and show a naive readiness
       to attribute to God everything they hear in the name of
       Christianity. Don't do that. Believe God, but don't be-
       lieve everything you hear.

III. THE METHOD (vv. 2-6a)

How do we test the spirits? Ask three questions: Do they confess the divine Lord? Do they possess the divine life? Do they
profess the divine law? That can be reduced to three words: incarnation, regeneration, and revelation.

A. Confess the Divine Lord (vv. 2-3)

    1. The criterion of the confession (v. 2)

       "By this know ye the Spirit of God; every spirit that
       confesseth that Jesus Christ is come in the flesh is of
       God."

The word translated "confesseth" is in the present tense, referring to everyone who continues to confess. The word translated "confesseth" (Gk., *homologeō*) means "to say the same." Everyone who continually says the same thing about Jesus that God said about Him is from God. To confess your sin means to say the same thing that God says about your sin. A true teacher from the Holy Spirit must agree with God's revelation about Jesus Christ. If he doesn't, his source is demonic. You may think a false teacher is nice, but he's not if Satan is going to deceive you through him. Beware of a religion that talks about God but doesn't believe that Christ is God. That is a demonic religion according to 1 John 4:2-3. Only those who believe Jesus Christ is God in human flesh are of God. Verse 3 says, "Every spirit that confesseth not . . . is not of God."

Confessing Christ as Lord

First John 4:2 says, "Every spirit that confesseth that Jesus Christ is come in the flesh is of God." In the Greek text, there is no word for "that." A good way to translate verse 2 is: "Every spirit who is continuing to say the same thing about Jesus as Christ come in the flesh is of God." A Christian believes that the human Jesus and the divine God are one and the same. But even the demons recognize Christ's identity:

1. Mark 1:24—As Jesus came across a demon-possessed man, the demon said, "Let us alone! What have we to do with thee, thou Jesus of Nazareth? Art thou come to destroy us? I know thee, who thou art, the Holy One of God."

2. Mark 3:11—"Unclean spirits, when they saw him, fell down before him, and cried, saying, Thou art the Son of God." Demons can make a propositional confession.

3. Mark 5:7—Jesus met a maniac who carried inside him a legion of demons (cf. Luke 8:28). One demon cried out, "What have I to do with thee, Jesus, thou Son of the Most High God?"

4. Acts 19:13-15—Certain unbelievers were trying to imitate Paul by casting out demons. An evil spirit replied, "Jesus I know, and Paul I know; but who are ye?"

However, it's one thing to make a statement about Jesus Christ; it's quite another to have Him as Lord of your life. When you test the spirits, find out if the person is confessing Jesus *is* Lord or confessing Jesus *as* Lord. Salvation comes only by confessing Christ as Lord (Rom. 10:9-10).

a) Commitment to the lordship of Christ

The incarnation is a basic truth. When someone says he is a teacher sent from God, I want to know if he confesses that Jesus is God incarnate and acknowledges Him as Lord of his life.

b) Commitment to the deity of Christ

Jesus is the Greek form of the Hebrew name Joshua, which means "Jehovah saves." So 1 John 4:2 implies confessing that Jesus is Jehovah. *Christ* means "the anointed one." So the Jehovah of the Old Testament is the incarnate Messiah of the New Testament. Jesus is God. Romans 5:8 says Christ died for our sins. First John 3:16 says God died for our sins. Christ and God are the same.

2. The criterion of the denial (v. 3)

"Every spirit that confesseth not that Jesus Christ is come in the flesh is not of God; and this is that spirit of antichrist, of which ye have heard that it should come, and even now already is it in the world."

The Antichrist is not just a man; it is a system of opposition to Christ. Sometimes Satan is openly opposed to Christ, and sometimes he tries to be the substitute for Christ. Anyone who doesn't believe that Jesus is God in human flesh is fueled by the Antichrist.

John says, "Ye have heard that it should come." When did the people hear that? They could have heard it through Daniel (7:8; 11:36-45), but I believe John is referring to previous apostolic teaching. The apostles believed the Antichrist was coming. The first epistle of John wasn't written until late in the first century,

95

whereas the Thessalonian epistles were written by Paul much earlier. No doubt the people had read those epistles, which outline the career of the Antichrist.

John, however, didn't limit the word to a single man (see p. 12). First John 2:18 says, "It is the last time; and as ye have heard that antichrist shall come, even now are there many antichrists." Everyone who is in opposition to or who tries to take the place of Christ is an antichrist. There will be a final Antichrist, but the opposition of antichrists already exists in the world.

B. Possess the Divine Life (v. 4)

"Ye are of God, little children, and have overcome them, because greater is he that is in you, than he that is in the world."

The Holy Spirit is greater and more powerful than the devil. You possess the Holy Spirit. Verse 4 affirms the security of the believer against false teachers.

1. The source of believers

Verse 4 says, "Ye are of God, little children." Believers have God as their source. They have been born of God and are "partakers of the divine nature" (2 Pet. 1:4). We possess the incorruptible seed (1 John 3:9).

2. The security of believers

The Holy Spirit keeps us from being seduced by demons. First John 2:20 says, "Ye have an [anointing] from the Holy One, and ye know all things." God has given us the Holy Spirit as permanent protection against false doctrine. Verse 21 says, "I have not written unto you because ye know not the truth, but because ye know it." Since we have the Holy Spirit, we know the truth. Verse 27 says, "The anointing which ye have received of him abideth in you, and ye need not that any man teach you; but as the same anointing teacheth you of all things, and is truth, and is no lie, and even as it hath taught you, ye shall abide in him." A Christian will continue to abide in Christ because the Holy Spirit will never allow him to be seduced by false doctrine. You can overcome false teachers because the Holy Spirit is stronger than the devil.

The Magnetic Christian

Regeneration provides believers with an affinity for the truth. As a child I owned a magnet with metal shavings attached. I used to enjoy putting the shavings in a pile of dirt and then running the magnet across the dirt. Only that which had an affinity to the magnet came out of the pile; the dirt remained. A Christian is like a magnet. As he moves about the earth, the truth of God attaches to him because he has an affinity for it. The Holy Spirit draws the truth of God to the Christian and rejects the rest.

First John 4:4 is an implied test. If a man is a true teacher of God, his life will be transformed by the Holy Spirit, and he will have an affinity for God's truth. When faced with some teacher who claims to be from God, ask these questions: Does the Holy Spirit appear to be at work in his life? Does he love and obey the Word of God? False teachers will fail this test because they aren't regenerate.

C. Profess the Divine Law (vv. 5-6a)

If a person is of the spirit of truth, he will declare God's Word.

1. Demonic mouthpieces (v. 5)

"They are of the world; therefore speak they of the world, and the world heareth them."

False teachers are a part of the world—a reference to Satan's evil system. False teachers speak about the system because they are of the system. And the system therefore listens to them. The beginning of verse 5 in the Greek text is an *ablative of source,* telling us that the source of false teachers is Satan. Demons always accommodate their teaching to the world. They aim at whatever is popular. There are enough religious systems to accommodate every mentality. Mormonism, for example, appeals to someone who is self-righteous. Then there's the opposite—religious systems that appeal to the corrupt. There's something for everyone. Different demons operate behind different systems. The system propagates what Satan dictates, and the world hears it.

2. Godly mouthpieces (v. 6a)

"We are of God. He that knoweth God heareth us; he that is not of God heareth not us."

a) The source of Christian doctrine

Compare verses 4 and 6. Whereas in verse 4 John is talking about the source of our life, here he's talking about the source of our teaching. We are of God—we speak of God, and he who knows God hears what we say. The third test is the profession of divine law. Does the teacher declare and affirm God's Word? If someone says, "This is the truth," I say, "Do you believe Scripture in total?"

The word *we* in verse 6 has primary reference to the apostles, for they were the main writers of the New Testament. What they wrote was inspired by God.

b) The standard of Christian doctrine

If you want to know if someone is a true teacher, find out if he teaches the Word of God and if God's people are listening to what he says. You don't want to listen to someone whom no one else is listening to. Be suspect of anyone who publishes all his material from a secret press. If there is any credibility to what he says, someone will be propagating it. Isaiah 8:20 says, "To the law and to the testimony; if they speak not according to this word, it is because there is no light in them." If someone makes a spiritual claim that isn't in the Bible, don't believe it. If someone claims to have had a vision, don't believe that either. God's teachers speak God's Word, and God's people hear them.

The complete Old and New Testaments are the sole standard by which all teaching, oral and written, is to be tested. So before you accept a teaching, find out if it's biblical. Can you quote a chapter and verse on the teaching? If you can't, you don't want to listen, because there's no new revelation. Are God's people listening to the teacher? I'm not referring to people who don't know any better; I'm referring to those who do—the Bible scholars and students. When someone claims to have made a new discovery, check it out against God's Word.

IV. THE APPLICATION (v. 6b)

"By this know we the spirit of truth, and the spirit of error."

Let's apply the test:

A. Confessing the Divine Lord—Incarnation

1. Christian Scientists say Jesus was a mere man who possessed the Christ Spirit, which is ideal truth.

2. Jehovah's Witnesses say Jesus was a created individual and is the second greatest personage of the universe. They think He was a god but not almighty God, whom they call Jehovah.

3. Theosophists say Jesus is a man who taught good ideas.

4. Mormons say Jesus is one of many sub-gods.

5. Unitarians say Jesus is not God, and they deny the Trinity.

6. Modernists say Jesus was a great ethical teacher.

Each group is as demonic as the other.

B. Possessing the Divine Life—Regeneration

If all the teachers who claim to be sent from God are true, then they ought to manifest some evidence of a regenerated life. Yet if you study the leaders of the false religious

99

systems you will find that none of them can pass the test of biblical morality. Read about the lives of Brigham Young, Joseph Smith, Mary Baker Eddy, and Judge Rutherford. They lived vile and corrupt lives. A person propagating a demonic religion is going to lead a demonic existence. Second Peter 2:12 says false teachers are "natural brute beasts." Verse 13 says, "Spots they are and blemishes."

C. Professing the Divine Word—Revelation

When people say they teach the truth, I want to know if they teach the Bible alone. What does Christian Science have? The Bible plus *Science and Health with Key to the Scriptures.* What does Mormonism have? The Bible plus The Book of Mormon among others. Every false system has the Bible plus something, or they don't believe the Bible at all. Anything minus or plus the Bible is demonic.

When you apply the tests, false teachers and their systems become evident.

Focusing on the Facts

1. What four words describe the essence of false doctrine (see pp. 86-87)?
2. Who are some of the people in the Bible who warned believers about false doctrine (see pp. 87-88)?
3. Who is the source of false doctrine (see p. 88)?
4. What was the first doctrine taught by demons (see pp. 88-89)?
5. Explain how people can be influenced to believe in an idol (1 Cor. 10:19-20; see p. 89).
6. What is the biggest problem Christians have with false teachers (2 Pet. 2:1; see p. 91)?
7. What is the twofold command John gives in 1 John 4:1 (see p. 92)?
8. According to 1 John 4:1, why should believers test the spirits (see p. 92)?
9. What three questions should believers answer in determining the validity of teachers who claim they speak God's truth (see p. 93)?
10. Explain the kind of confession John is referring to in 1 John 4:2 (see pp. 93-94).

11. What is involved in confessing Christ (1 John 4:2; see p. 95)?
12. Who is greater and more powerful than the devil (1 John 4:4; see p. 96)?
13. Explain how a Christian is like a magnet (see p. 97).
14. Why do demons aim their false doctrine at whatever is popular in the world (1 John 4:5; see pp. 97-98)?
15. What two things about a teacher's doctrine will reveal if he speaks God's truth (see p. 98)?

Pondering the Principles

1. What significance does 1 John 4:4 have in your life? Thank God for supplying you with the Holy Spirit as your protector from false doctrine. Thank Him for teaching you the truth so that you can identify error. To encourage yourself, memorize 1 John 4:4: "Ye are of God, little children, and have overcome them, because greater is he that is in you, than he that is in the world."

2. Perhaps you've heard a particular teacher you've become somewhat suspicious of. If so, apply the tests you learned from this study. Examine his teaching. Does he confess Jesus *as* Lord? Remember, he doesn't pass this part of the test if he only acknowledges that Jesus *is* Lord. Next, find out if his life manifests the fruit of the Spirit. Does he walk in obedience to God's Word? You may have to do some research into his life and ministry. Finally, determine if he teaches and affirms God's Word. Is his teaching biblical, and are God's people listening to what he says? When you finish applying the tests, you will know if he is of the spirit of truth or the spirit of error.

6
Why We Should Love One Another

Outline

Introduction
A. The Unfulfilled Love of the World
B. The Fulfilled Love of Christianity
   1. Regarded as perfect
   2. Realized in obedience
     a) 1 John 2:5
     b) 1 John 5:3

Lesson
I. Love Is the Essence of God (vv. 7-8)
  A. Present in His Children (v. 7)
  B. Absent from His Enemies (v. 8)
    1. The cooperation of God's love
     a) Creation
     b) Volition
     c) Providence
     d) Redemption
     e) Eternal life
    2. The character of God's love
     a) It is unconditional
     b) It is tough
     c) It is compassionate
II. Love Was Manifested by Christ (vv. 9-11)
  A. The Expression of God's Love (vv. 9-10)
    1. Christ's supreme act
    2. Christ's supreme role
    3. Christ's supreme sacrifice
  B. The Example of God's Love (v. 11)
    1. The pattern
    2. The principle

Introduction

A. The Unfulfilled Love of the World

I am amazed at how much of secular music deals with the subject of love. However, the love expressed in those songs is basically unfulfilled. There seems to be a lost-ness—a love that never has any ultimate meaning. Compare that with divine love. The only conclusion is that human love is unfulfilled. At best it's imperfect.

Philosopher Jean Paul Sartre wrote a novel entitled *Nausea*. Roquentin, his main character, tries to find the meaning of life. He looks in many places and decides to give love a try. But all he knows is mechanical and meaningless sex. He concludes that man is egoistic and loves only to enslave his lover. Roquentin is so unfulfilled in love that the nausea of life becomes overwhelming. He says he contemplated killing himself in order to remove one more superfluous life.

B. The Fulfilled Love of Christianity

People long for a love that is perfect, complete, and fulfilling. First John 4 is the record of that kind of love. Verse 12
says, "No man hath seen God at any time. If we love one
another, God dwelleth in us, and his love is perfected in
us." Verse 17 says, "Herein is our love made perfect."
Verse 18 says, "There is no fear in love, but perfect love
casteth out fear." Perfect love is available to men.

The New Testament uses many adjectives to describe the
love of God: brotherly, unfeigned, believing, serving,
abounding, forgiving, comforting, and laboring. But the
greatest description is perfect love.

1. Regarded as perfect

What does John mean when he says love is perfect? In
English we think of something that has no flaws. But
the Greek word *teleioō* refers to something that is fulfilled. It means "completion" or "wholeness." When Jesus was on the cross He said, "It is finished" (John
19:30). He used a form of the same word. He finished
the work God had committed to Him. John uses the
word in the perfect passive, denoting the completeness
of love in the life of an individual. There is available a
love that is whole—a love that is the best it can possibly
be in the human realm. It is not necessarily flawless in
this life because we bring in flaws as a result of our humanness. Romans 5:5 says, "The love of God is shed
abroad in our hearts." God has committed His love to
us.

2. Realized in obedience

God's love realizes its perfection in us only when we
obey the Word of God.

a) 1 John 2:5—"Whosoever keepeth his word, in him
verily is the love of God perfected." The obedient individual realizes the fullness of all that God's love
means.

b) 1 John 5:3—"This is the love of God, that we keep his commandments." Fulfilling love is not sentiment or mystical experience; it is contingent upon moral obedience.

The workings of perfect love are detailed in 1 John 4:7-21. That is John's third and last discussion of love in his letter. His two previous discussions were in 1 John 2:7-11 and 3:10-14. Love is the soul-searching, moral test of true Christianity. When someone claims to be a Christian, John says we're to find out if he loves his brothers and sisters in Christ.

First John 4:7 is the key to the passage: "Beloved, let us love one another." Verse 12 says, "If we love one another." And verse 21 closes the passage: "This commandment have we from him, that he who loveth God love his brother also." The beginning, middle, and ending of this passage deal with loving one another. The first word in verse 7 is "beloved" (Gk., *agapetoi*, "divinely loved ones"). John is saying, "Since God loves you, let us love one another." That is one more use of the present tense to denote habitual action. Christians are to habitually love one another. Now when the Word of God says something once, it's divine truth. When it says something twice, that means it's important. But when the Word of God says the same thing over and over, we'd better pay particular attention. God repeats the theme of love so much because we can easily forget to love. We need to be reminded to have a perfect, complete, and fulfilled love for one another. John gives several reasons for loving one another.

Lesson

I. LOVE IS THE ESSENCE OF GOD (vv. 7-8)

A. Present in His Children (v. 7)

"Beloved, let us love one another; for love is of God, and everyone that loveth is born of God, and knoweth God."

We ought to love one another because love is a characteristic of God. Since we are God's children, we should reflect the character of our Father. Those of you with children

106

may have had someone say to you, "Your kids are just like you." A child will take on the traits of his parents, both from the standpoint of heredity and environment. We are born of God—that's our heredity; and we have experienced His presence in our lives—our environment. God's people are to bear His resemblance.

Change Your Name or Change Your Behavior

It is said that a soldier in the army of Alexander the Great had misbehaved. As he came before the judgment seat, the presiding judge asked him his name. He said, "It is Alexander, the same as Alexander the Great." The judge replied, "Change your name or change your behavior." Do you name the name of Christ? If so, you ought to act like Him. Otherwise you bring reproach on His name. If we are the children of God, we should manifest His love. Everyone who habitually loves gives evidence of being born of God. Since love has God as its source, those who display that love give evidence of being born of God.

The phrase "everyone that loveth is born of God" (v. 7) should be rendered "everyone that loveth has been begotten of God." That is a past action with continuous results. Remember, John is attacking the heretical teaching of the Gnostics. In verse 7 he points out that it isn't those who claim to know God who are true, but those who love that give evidence of being born of God.

B. Absent from His Enemies (v. 8)

"He that loveth not knoweth not God; for God is love."

It doesn't matter what someone claims—if he doesn't love, he doesn't know God. The Gnostics knew a lot of speculative theology and had a superficial knowledge of Scripture, but they didn't know God because they didn't love others. They had so elevated themselves by their intellectual attainments that they had contempt for everyone who supposedly knew less than they did. They were the opposite of love.

1. The cooperation of God's love

God is love. However, love does not define God; God defines love. All God's activities are expressed in love because all His attributes work in cooperation. Even in judgment God's love shines through. To prove that, ask yourself, Where is God's judgment the most demonstrative? At the cross, where He poured out His wrath on His own Son as the punishment for sin. But where is God's love displayed most? At the cross, where His justice and love operate together.

That God is love explains the following:

a) Creation

Why would God create a world that brings Him so much trouble? Because God is love, and love does not exist in isolation.

b) Volition

God gave man volition because a love relationship necessitates the ability to choose.

c) Providence

Since God is love, His creative act was followed by His constant care. His love sustains and upholds the world. He makes the rain to fall on the just and the unjust (Matt. 5:45).

d) Redemption

If God cared only about the law, He would leave man to the consequences of his sin. But because God is love, He seeks to save. Love provides a remedy.

e) Eternal life

Why will believers be in heaven forever? Because God loves them and wants them to be there with Him.

It Can Be Hard to Believe That God Is Love

Some people find it hard to believe that God is love. They say, "If God is a God of love, how can He allow so much injustice in the world?" The back cover of John Wenham's book *The Goodness of God* (Downers Grove, Ill.: InterVarsity, 1974), reads: "Look at the world around us: History is a long tale of man's inhumanity to man. Spain had its Inquisition, Britain its Atlantic slave trade, Germany its gas chambers, Russia its Siberian labor camps, the United States its Indian reservations. And the world is still swept by fear and lust, greed and racial tension.

"Nature too seems twisted. Babies are born deformed. They inherit diseases and tendencies to insanity. Ours is a world of preying animals, parasites, viruses and bacteria."

Wenham writes, "Easy answers could not possibly be right. . . . We [must] realize that we are children, that we are fools, that we are at heart conceited, stiff-necked rebels, who will get everything wrong, unless we are prepared to give up telling God what he should be like and what he should do" (p. 10).

Objectors simply tell us what sin has done, not what God has done. People ask, "If God is a God of love, why doesn't He stop all the wars?" The obvious answer is He didn't start them. The Word of God says God is love. I believe it. All you have to do to prove it is look at the cross.

2. The character of God's love

   a) It is unconditional

   There are no conditions to God's love. He loves everyone equally.

   b) It is tough

   When many people think of someone who is loving, they think of someone who doesn't cause turmoil. But that's not true. Parents love their children, yet they discipline them. God loves us but does not indulge us.

c) It is compassionate

> In Jeremiah 13:13-16 God tells the people He will destroy them if they don't change their behavior and give Him glory. Then in verse 17 He says, "But if ye will not hear it . . . mine eye shall weep bitterly." He feels for His people and wants what's best for them.

> By nature God is love. If we are His children, we will love. Our love will be unconditional—no one will have to earn it, and it will be available to all. Our love will be tough and not indulgent. Love does not tolerate sin; it rebukes sin. Our love will be like God's—it will be compassionate even in judgment.

Ephesians 5:1 says, "Be ye, therefore, followers of God, as dear children." God is our Father; we are to manifest His character. Verse 2 says to "walk in love." Why? Because that manifests God's character. We are to do that which manifests God.

II. LOVE WAS MANIFESTED BY CHRIST (vv. 9-11)

A. The Expression of God's Love (vv. 9-10)

> "In this was manifested the love of God toward us, that God sent his only begotten Son into the world, that we might live through him. Herein is love, not that we loved God, but that he loved us, and sent his Son to be the propitiation for our sins."

We are to love one another based on God's gift to us: His Son. The origin of love is in the being of God; the manifestation of God is in the coming of Christ.

1. Christ's supreme act

> There have been many manifestations of God's love, but the greatest is the death of Christ. Romans 5:8 says, "God commendeth his love toward us in that, while we were yet sinners, Christ died for us."

2. Christ's supreme role

   John says Christ is God's "only begotten [Gk., *mono-genēs*] Son." What does that mean? It does not refer only to Christ's birth or His humanness. Here it means "the supreme one." There is none greater than Christ. He is God's unspeakable gift (2 Cor. 9:15).

3. Christ's supreme sacrifice

   To provide life for us, Christ had to become "the propitiation for our sin" (1 John 4:10). God is a God of justice, who cannot tolerate sin. The Greek word translated "propitiation" is *hilasmos*, which means "satisfaction." Christ's death satisfied God's requirements for dealing with sin. Hebrews 9:5 translates a form of that word as "mercy seat." In Old Testament times, blood from a sacrifice was taken into the Holy of Holies once a year and poured out on the Mercy Seat. That satisfied God's righteous requirements.

B. The Example of God's Love (v. 11)

   "Beloved, if God so loved us, we ought also to love one another."

   1. The pattern

      God gave us the example of Christ to follow. In John 13:34 Jesus says, "Love one another; as I have loved you." How has He loved us? By giving Himself in self-sacrifice. That's how we're to love one another.

   2. The principle

      Ephesians 5:1-2 says, "Be ye, therefore, followers of God, as dear children; and walk in love, as Christ also hath loved us, and hath given himself for us an offering and a sacrifice." How are we to love? In the same self-sacrificing manner that Christ loved. Love is not an emotion; it is an act of self-sacrifice. It takes no effort to say, "I love you." John addresses that issue in 1 John 3:18: "My little children, let us not love in word, neither in tongue, but in deed and in truth." We are to love as Christ loved—we are called to make sacrifices for each other. First John 3:17 says, "Whosoever hath this world's good, and seeth his brother have need, and shutteth up his compassions from him, how dwelleth the love of God in him?" That verse defines love as simply giving to someone who has a need. We're to love each other sacrificially.

III. LOVE IS THE CHRISTIAN'S TESTIMONY (v. 12)

A. The Invisible Glory of God (v. 12a)

"No man hath seen God at any time."

When someone says he has had a vision of God, you can tell him that no man has seen God at any time. John 4:24 says, "God is a Spirit." Jesus said, "A spirit hath not flesh and bones" (Luke 24:39).

1. Unseen by Moses

Some object, saying Moses saw God in Exodus 33:22. But God Himself told Moses, "No man [shall] see me, and live" (v. 20). Moses saw only a manifestation of God reduced to visible light. Similarly the Son of God unveiled His flesh at the mount of transfiguration and gave His disciples a brief glimpse of His glory (Matt. 17:2). God is light (1 John 1:5), and there is no way in which anyone could ever gaze into absolute light without being totally consumed. No man has ever seen God in His entirety.

2. Unseen by Isaiah

Scripture tells us Isaiah saw "the Lord sitting upon a throne high and lifted up" (Isa. 6:1). He may have seen a representation of God, but he didn't see the unveiled God. First Timothy 1:17 says God is invisible.

If God can't be seen at all, the only hope the world has of recognizing God is for Him to become visible in human

112

flesh. And that's just what He did. John 1:14 says, "The Word was made flesh, and dwelt among us (and we beheld his glory, the glory as of the only begotten of the Father), full of grace and truth." God chose the body of the Lord Jesus Christ to manifest Himself. But He also chose another type of body.

B. The Visible Manifestation of God (v. 12*b*)

"If we love one another, God dwelleth in us, and his love is perfected in us."

Scripture says the church is the Body of Christ (Eph. 4:12). We are to manifest the invisible God to the world. How will the world see Him? When we love one another. In John 13:34-35 Jesus says, "A new commandment I give unto you, that ye love one another. . . . By this shall all men know that ye are my disciples." The revelation of God exists through the love of the church. Is it any wonder the world is having difficulty figuring out where God went? We have a tremendous responsibility, but we fall short of it. Love is our strongest apologetic.

I was approached by someone who said, "I'm very concerned about someone at Grace Church. I don't see love in his life. All I see is bitterness, a critical spirit, and hatred. He tosses unkind words toward others. I'm not too sure he's even a Christian." Now I don't know whether he is a Christian or not, but it's certainly not hard to tell when love isn't present. Why? Because love is the manifestation of the indwelling of God. When I love my brother, God's love is perfected in me.

Jesus isn't physically present in this world; He's seated at the right hand of the Father (Heb. 1:3). The church is the collective representation of God in this world. That's why our testimony is critical. Our love is that testimony.

IV. LOVE IS THE CHRISTIAN'S ASSURANCE (vv. 13-16)

One ongoing struggle Christians have is doubting their salvation. You may ask certain Christians if they have ever invited Christ into their lives, and they will say, "Yes! Thirteen times in the last week." We like to sing hymns such as "Blessed Assurance" so we can feel better.

Believers can be assured of their salvation when they see deeds of love manifest in their lives. First John 3:18-19 says, "My little children, let us not love in word, neither in tongue, but in deed and in truth. By this we know that we are of the truth, and shall assure our hearts before him." When you can see visible evidence of love in your life, then you know God is in it. Continual deeds of love are evidence of salvation. Your love brings about your assurance.

A. The Presence of the Holy Spirit (v. 13)

"By this know we that we dwell in him, and he in us, because he hath given us of his Spirit."

The first confirmation we have is the presence of the Holy Spirit in our hearts crying, "Abba, Father" (Rom. 8:15). Romans 8:16 says, "The Spirit himself beareth witness with our spirit, that we are the children of God." The Holy Spirit is our witness.

B. The Confession of Jesus Christ (vv. 14-15)

"We have seen and do testify that the Father sent the Son to be the Savior of the world. Whosoever shall confess that Jesus is the Son of God, God dwelleth in him, and he in God."

The first guarantee of your salvation is the presence of the Holy Spirit, and the second is your belief that Jesus is God in human flesh. Someone said to me, "I don't know if I'm a Christian." I asked him if he believed Jesus is God and if he had ever been prompted by the Holy Spirit. Romans 8:14 says, "As many as are led by the Spirit of God, they are the sons of God." The Holy Spirit doesn't lead unsaved people.

C. The Manifestation of God's Love (v. 16)

"We have known and believed the love that God hath to us. God is love, and. he that dwelleth in love dwelleth in God, and God in him."

The third and climactic confirmation of your salvation is the love of God manifested in your life. Satan does not produce deeds of love in believers.

V. LOVE IS THE CHRISTIAN'S CONFIDENCE (vv. 17-18)

A. Perfect Love Produces Boldness (v. 17)

1. Absence of fear (v. 17a)

"Herein is our love made perfect, that we may have boldness in the day of judgment."

"Day of judgment" is a general term. I don't think we can restrict it to the rapture, the *bēma* judgment, or the great white throne judgment. The point is we don't need to worry—we will have boldness when the time comes because we've seen perfect love manifested in our lives. The Greek word translated "boldness" is *parrēsia*, which means "confidence." We have confidence in the future. When love is made perfect in our lives, we don't fear the coming of Christ.

A Phony Rapture

Some Christians don't want Jesus to return because they're afraid of the rapture. They're worried they'll be left behind. That reminds me of one of the dumber things I participated in while in college. One guy was terrified of the rapture, so the rest of us in the dormitory decided to pull off a fake rapture. We went to the soundstage and picked up a large aluminum sheet that made thunderclaps. We borrowed a trumpet and a press camera with a large flash. Then we prepared the rooms around his. We caved in the pillows and tucked in the covers of the beds. In the middle of the night we went into his room while he was asleep in his bunk. One guy held the camera right over his face. One hit the aluminum sheet, another blew the trumpet, and someone yelled out, "Come!" As he opened his eyes, the flash went off, blinding him. Then we all hid down the hall. He came wandering out of his room and went into one room and then another. Then he came screaming down the hall, "I'm left! I'm left!" We tried to justify our fun as a lesson to teach him that such fear was foolish.

a) The fear of some

> Some people don't want to come to the *bēma* because they're afraid they won't receive any rewards. They think all they have accomplished is wood, hay, and stubble, which will be consumed (1 Cor. 3:12-13). My grandfather wrote this in his Bible: "When I stand at the judgment seat of Christ and He shows me His plan for me—the plan of my life as it might have been—and I see how I blocked Him here and checked Him there and would not yield my will, will there be grief in my Savior's eyes—grief though He loves me still? He would have me rich, but I stand here poor, stripped of all but His grace while memory runs like a hunted thing down a path I can't retrace. Then my desolate heart will well nigh break with tears I cannot shed. I will cover my face with my empty hands; I will bow my uncrowned head."

b) The confidence of others

> Actually, there is no need for a Christian to worry. Every man will have his reward (1 Cor. 3:8). I like the attitude of Paul, who said he and other believers "love his appearing" (2 Tim. 4:8). Do you know why Paul had such confidence? Because he had the kind of visible love that gives a believer confidence.

2. Union with Christ (v. 17*b*)

"Because as he is, so are we in this world."

God has made us one with Christ. Romans 8:1 says, "There is, therefore, now no condemnation to them who are in Christ Jesus." But you'll never have security, even though you may know your theology, unless you can see visible deeds of love in your life.

B. Perfect Love Eliminates Fear (v. 18)

"There is no fear in love, but perfect love casteth out fear, because fear hath punishment. He that feareth is not made perfect in love."

If you're afraid, then your love is not yet perfect. Love that is mature and fulfilled has no fear of punishment—only confidence. Because you love your brothers and sisters in Christ, you can look forward to the coming of Christ.

VI. LOVE IS REASONABLE (vv. 19-20)

A. The Progression of Love (v. 19)

"We love him, because he first loved us."

We have the ability to love each other because God manifested His love to us in Christ and then placed His love in us through the Holy Spirit. It is logical for the Christian to love in response.

B. The Pretenders of Love (v. 20)

"If a man says, I love God, and hateth his brother, he is a liar; for he that loveth not his brother, whom he hath seen, how can he love God, whom he hath not seen?"

This is the seventh time John has used the phrase "if a man says." Each time it refers to some illegitimate claim to faith. It is a warning against some pretender. In this case someone claims to love God, yet he hates his brother. Where does God dwell in this world? In us. How can I love God and hate another believer when God lives in that believer? It's impossible.

I don't care how obnoxious another Christian may seem, God still lives in him. Don't say you love God but hate a believer. How can you claim to love the invisible God and not love His presence in His people? It is easier to serve a visible man than an invisible God. If you can't serve a visible man, you certainly can't serve the invisible God. A claim to love God is an obvious lie if it is not accompanied by unselfish love for our brothers and sisters in Christ.

Conclusion

John sums up his thoughts in verse 21: "This commandment have we from him, that he who loveth God love his brother also." Don't say you love God if you don't love your brother. We are to love because love is the essence of God's nature. We are His children, and we are partakers of the divine nature. We should love because that is a manifestation of Christ, and He is our example. We should love because that is the Christian's testimony, assurance, and confidence. Love is the only reasonable option for believers.

How Does God's Love Function?

1. It is unrequited

   Christian love doesn't need anything in return. It doesn't say, "I love you because you love me." One person doesn't love someone because he does him favors. He loves him independent of any return.

2. It is unconditional

   Love doesn't care how much it is offended, abused, and sinned against. We need to forgive and forget. There are no conditions to perfect love.

3. It is vicarious

   Love gladly bears the pain of others. We should be willing to bear one another's burdens, weeping with those who weep and rejoicing with those who rejoice.

4. It is self-giving

   Love is synonymous with sacrifice. If I have one meal and two of us need food, I should give it to you and go without.

5. It is righteous

   Love does not tolerate sin. When my child sins, I discipline him. When a believer sins, the church disciplines him. When you truly love someone, you will point out his sins to him in a loving manner.

God's love for us was unrequited—He loved us when we hated Him. It is unconditional—it didn't matter to Him what we had done: He forgave all of it. His love is vicarious—He substituted His Son in our place. His love is self-giving—He made the ultimate sacrifice. He gave His supreme gift: His Son. Finally, His love is righteous—He loves us and therefore chastens us. Let's follow His example by loving one another.

Focusing on the Facts

1. What are some of the adjectives the New Testament uses to describe the love of God (see p. 105)?
2. What does John mean when he describes love as perfect (see p. 105)?
3. What must happen before love can be perfected in believers (see p. 105)?
4. According to 1 John 4:7, why should believers love one another (see p. 107)?
5. Which is correct: love defines God, or God defines love (see p. 108)?
6. What does knowing that God is love explain (see p. 108)?
7. Describe the character of God's love (see pp. 109-10).
8. What basic principle is stated by Ephesians 5:1 (see p. 110)?
9. What is the greatest manifestation of God's love (see p. 111)?
10. What does "propitiation" mean in 1 John 4:10 (see p. 111)?
11. What pattern are believers to follow in their practice of love (see p. 111)?
12. Why can't God be seen (John 4:24; see p. 112)?
13. In what two ways is God made visible to the world (see pp. 112-13)?
14. What ongoing struggle is experienced by many Christians (see p. 113)?
15. According to 1 John 4:13-16, what three aspects of the Christian life provide assurance for the believer (see pp. 114-15)?
16. Why can believers have confidence in the day of judgment (see p. 115)?
17. Why do some believers fear the rapture (see pp. 115-16)?
18. According to 1 John 4:19, why do Christians love (see p. 117)?

19. When is a claim to love God an obvious lie (1 John 4:20; see p. 117)?
20. Describe God's love (see pp. 118-19).

Pondering the Principles

1. Read through 1 John. Record each passage that discusses obedience. How many of those verses relate to love? Based on what you have read, what do you need to do to see love perfected in your life? Is love being perfected in your life, or is disobedience preventing that from happening? What areas of your life need to be more aligned with God's standard before you will manifest perfect love? Make the commitment to institute changes today.

2. Our love should be like God's love—unrequited, unconditional, vicarious, self-giving, and righteous. On a scale of 1-10, rate the degree that each characteristic is displayed in your life. What are your strengths? What are your weaknesses? Begin to work on improving your weakest characteristic. What are some things you can do to make improvements in the other areas? Ask God to give you guidance in the application of those things.

Scripture Index

Topical Index